NORTH CAROLINA
STATE BOARD OF COMMUNITY COLLEGES
LIBRARIES
ASHEVILLE-BUNCOMBE TECHNICAL COLL

S0-BYS-443

Discarded
Date SEP 1 7 2024

Dollhouse stove with owner

This book belongs to:

the art and ingenuity of the
woodstove

Written, designed, and illustrated by
jan adkins

Everest House
Publishers   New York

Copyright© 1978 by Jan Adkins

Though a reviewer may quote this book to the extent of a line or two, no further part may be reproduced or stored by any means, electronic or mechanical

Printed in the United States of America

This book is for two fine friends:

Marilyn Marlowe and Perry Knowlton

contents

Very simply, it takes a fire to make a home. A fire makes a center, a pivot of warmth and light around which life revolves. Fire is our old friend, our first ally against the cold and damp which threaten us. Wild animals flee from it, but dogs, our second allies, are comfortable with it, and cats join us to decorate our hearths.

Fire gave us comfort beyond the weather's chances. It made homes of our lairs, it gave us roots. It made a shell of comfort away from necessity, and within that glowing egg of warmth, a rude and hardly viable species began to look inward and reason with its fears. The power and comfort of fire gave us a self.

This was why Prometheus was punished. That he stole fire was nothing; he hid it in a tube and brought it to simple men and women foraging in the trees. The gods tortured him on the mountains because fire awakened the gods within man.

That fire, your fire, and the fire I sit before, are glints, reflections of the sun, they are captured bits of sunlight coaxed into freedom on our own altars. Our fires mark our homes over the earth, their delayed reflections lay out the pattern of civilization more plainly than the distant suns laid out the patterns of gods and dreads on the black, cold heavens.

Radiators full of hot water, openings that belch hot air and baseboards that click and creak with wattage are hot, but not warm. They make a place habitable but they do not make it home. A house with a furnace hidden in the cellar is removed from fire. A thermostat gives an electric order, there are mysterious rumblings in the cellar, and the room temperature increases. But the fire has lost its power. It cannot dispel gloom or drive out demons or set the imagination loose. Like all the powers given to us it has been harnessed, used, and banished into imbecile slavery.

Flame, immediate and alive, is a force we understand with that distant part of our nature which tenses in the autumn and quickens in the spring. We know fire: strong, wild and, in a pagan way, clean. It is a tool among our relics that has not lost its edge.

Melville says "Stand [a] man on his legs, set his feet a-going, and he will infallibly lead you to water." But stop him, tell him the sun is low and he must hunker down for the night, and he will lead you to fire or make one himself. Many people, seeing the sun setting on an age of cheap energy, have wandered back to the fire. For almost all of them the return to woodburning has been a reunion and not a retreat. Keeping warm has a new value for them that oil or gas or electric heat, all being so automatic, never had, and there are new pleasures.

It was inevitable that families would look to alternatives when oil and gas became scarce and expensive. It was just as certain that rural families would try woodburning and equally sure that they would be disappointed with most woodburners. Fireplaces and the potbellies and parlor stoves flaking away in the attics blazed briefly, consumed inordinate amounts of fuel for the heat

Railroad Lantern

8

they delivered and required constant tending. Wood burned uncontrollably in them and most of its heat warmed air rushing up the chimney.

There were, however, efficient woodstoves. They were the results of 200 years of thought and tinkering. Though they were not widely sold, the companies that built them had been supplying farms and cabins which were too far out for conventional heat for years. They were the native Ashleys and Riteways, looked on by city visitors as rural curiosities, like milking machines or hay balers, but they worked. There were also a few Scandanavian stoves in this country, developed and used in a cold climate where wood was scarce, a resource to be husbanded and used well.

These were "airtight" stoves, a title much brandished and little understood. They were stoves that had been designed and put together to restrict air inflow to one or two controllable inlets: the seams between plates were caulked so draughts could not enter, doors closed on gaskets to prevent an inrush all around the edge, cooking plates and draft controls were machined to make a tight fit. Air admitted to supply the firebox was regulated, so burning in the firebox was controlled. It was possible to set a fire, start it burning strongly, and then reduce its supply of air so that combustion continued at a slower, more efficient rate, with less heat lost up the flue, longer and more even heating from fewer logs.

If you shut your cat inside a cold stove, closed down, he will not be pleased but it is unlikely that he will suffocate. A better name for airtights would be "controlled draught" stoves. Their tightness, though not absolute, gives you control of the combusion rate. These are the stoves that make woodburning a workable heat source today.

Czechoslovakian tile stove

At our end of the twentieth century we are accustomed to hundreds of servants, electronic and mechanical slaves that respond to present needs. We have come to expect obedience from our environment. Our lives are padded and buffered against the effects of nature and of our own whims by the great expense of energy deployed haphazardly by those slaves and we continue to enjoy obedience but...at a price. Why would anyone abandon the convenience of thermostatically controlled heat for the admittedly involved job of heating with wood?

Heating with wood can be demanding, laborious, messy...it can be a real chore and no getting around it. But there are advantages to wood heat, philosophical and physical, that can outweigh the inconveniences.

Wood provides more than heat. There is a special quality to a stove's glow. It has direction; when you walk through the room you can feel the warmth change and play on your face and the backs of your hands. The stove's radiant heat warms surfaces and makes them pleasant to the touch. The well tended stove is constant in its

output and its heat is more even than the on-and-off furnace. The faint smell of woodsmoke and a hot stove is an attractive alternative to the clinging odor of gas or oil, and the atmosphere of a wood-heated home seems kinder to house plants than the trace-fumes in a gas- or oil-heated home.

In a small home or in a small-windowed room a stove is a surrogate for a view. A stove is a center for family life, a companion for talk and books; one can't imagine lying before a basement furnace reading *Treasure Island* to children. Whether a stove is ornate or severe it has presence, especially when it is giving off its warm glow; it centers a room, gives it a focal point of design. No design consideration is complete without noting the landscape effects of a well-ordered woodpile: that regular pattern of irregular shapes, speckled with a medley of similar shadings, is a strong influence outside.

Heating with wood, you are graphically aware of the direct tie between the earth and your comfort. You cut the wood, split it, stack it to dry, cart it, and then burn it for your warmth. There it is, laid out in a simple progression without the hid-

11

den mysteries of the Persian Gulf, supertankers, storage tanks, price manipulation, middlemen, and the groan of the oil truck in your driveway. The simplicity of it gives the responsibility for comfort to you, lays the pride of fending for yourself and your family in your hands. Your relationship with the earth through your own labor is strengthened. The best analogy may be Duncan Syme's, designer of the Vigilant and Defiant stoves: "The difference between automatic heat, gas or oil or electric, and wood heat is the difference between motoring and sailing." The whole process requires thought and planning, a feel for time and balance. Heating this way, like sailing, is a skill to be learned and perfected. Like a yawl or cutter, your stove is a complex tool needing attention and feeling. Heating with wood is a craft that can be turned to use, and though it is difficult, it has its own rewards. Wood heat can save you money, quite a substantial percentage of your fuel bill as things stand, but unless you are willing to learn the craft and accept the responsibilities, you had best take passage with the oil companies.

Wood heat has drawbacks and its own philosophical objections. We will discuss them later in the *Wood* section, but for those who are willing to trade work and thought for the mindless convenience of automatic heat, the jolly stove has a wealth of warm benefits.

Families warmed themselves before open fires at first. They may have heated stones in the fire and wrapped them in skins to warm their sleeping robes, much as churchgoers in the unheated worship houses of early America carried hot soapstones or coals in tin boxes into their pews and under their lap robes.

Early families may have built a fire against a flat rock propped up or against split, green planks to reflect heat into rock caves or skin tents.

It was convenient for later and more permanent dwellers to raise the fire on a hearth, to bring it up to working height. Cooking was done on spits, on thin, flat rocks, and even in fire-heated pits. (We have clambakes in similar ways.) When a roof was wanted, a hole was left open to vent the smoke. Certainly it must have been a smoky, dim atmosphere but the smoke itself was valuable. For example, Aborigines in New Guinea build rude sleeping platforms above and downwind of their fires to make a bug-proof envelope of smoke.

The Greeks gathered around braziers for heat and light and certainly cooked over open fires. Much later, grand houses of Spain had wheeled braziers like small wagons to move the heat source from room to room.

Roman designers and engineers began to apply principle to comfort. They reasoned that the smoke of a fire carried away most of its heat and they devised a way to use it. In the *hypocaust* a fire was built beneath heavy masonry in a room below the house or below a caldron for heating water in a bathhouse; the smoke was vented through channels under the floor covered by thin stonework and usually, mosaic; flues ran up through hollow walls and smoke emerged at the top of the house. The effect was surely pleasant, the floor warm to sandaled feet and radiant under

Roman brazier

14

togas. The hypocaust in similar form heats Chinese and Korean homes and there as in old Rome, its serious drawback is evident: insufficient draft, cracked masonry, green fuel and a number of other minor factors can combine to fill the heated space with carbon monoxide and snuff out the lives of the occupants. As thorough and thoughtful as the Romans were, it is odd that they never made a connection between mercury-ore lip rouge, lead pewter cooking pots, hypocausts, and their high rate of death and insanity.

history

Hypocaust

Few homes could afford such a complex heating system. The standard of heating for two thousand years was the open fire on a hearth and for a chimney, a simple hole in the roof. The mead halls of Denmark, the great halls of castles and keeps, and the crofters' homes were warmed by fires whose smoke collected among the blackened roof timbers before drifting out through a plain opening. One can surmise that a pall of bluish smoke hung like a ceiling over meals and feasts, its height varying with the wood, temperature, and humidity. Its smell would have invaded every stone and hanging and doublet, its fumes would have darkened furniture and tartans and dogs. Sweet rushes and herbs were spread on the floor to abate the smell. Perfumes, incense and spice cachets about the necks of highborn folks tried to alleviate it. The scent of wood heat would have clung to everyone, so pervasive as to be unnoticed.

As late as 1600 in the reign of Elizabeth I, chimneys were rare, things to be remarked about. Ladies and favored guests were given the few rooms served by flues. Even these fireplaces were smoky and erratic; later investigators—Count Rumford, Benjamin Franklin, Thomas Jefferson, and others—discovered that the proportions of a fireplace in height, width, depth, and the dimensions of its flue are crucially important.

In simpler homes mud and wattle chimneys were being built. These were clay, mud structures with a matrix of sticks and just as dangerous as they sound. The first fire in Boston in 1631 was probably due to one of these risky conveniences. As late as 1789, George Washington, in his travel diaries especially notes houses with brick and stone chimneys.

Let us note the problem of fire itself. It was

foot stove with tray
for hot coals

not until a hundred years ago that folks had such
an elegant thing as a match, or lucifers, as they
were called after their fiery, magic combustion.
Before these chemical wonders fire was produced
laboriously and uncertainly by friction with a fire
drill or grooved fire stick, or mechanically with
flint and steel. For the most part fire was pre-
served; villages kept a communal fire from which
citizens could fetch coals to rekindle their own
fires but every effort was made to keep the home
fire burning. Older brothers and sisters who
neglected their chore to bank the fire at night
probably caught a hot scolding over a cold hearth
in the morning. Travelers and musketeers
(before the flintlock) could carry fire only with a
slow burning punk wick called a slow match. In
Europe grenadiers used cigars to light bombs, just
as Conestoga wagon drivers in early Ohio rolled
long cigars to last between fires at post houses,
calling them stogies.

The desire to preserve the fire produced an
ancestor of the stove. In the less tolerant Middle
Ages, when the king's word was law, bells were
rung at nightfall and citizens were obliged to ex-
tinguish their lights and cover their fires. The
regulation was called *covrefeu* or "a covering of
the fire," which we now call *curfew*. Metal shells
of brass or tin, sometimes pierced in patterns,
which covered coals heaped against the fireplace
wall came also to be called covrefeus.

Some crude stoves are not much more complex than covrefeus which are only devices to limit
draft. Tent stoves from the Civil War covered
small campfires. Soldiers on bivouac adjusted the
draft by kicking more dirt up against a notch
around the bottom rim or pushing it away.

In Northern Europe houses were built
around great tile stoves. They were fueled

a curfew

through a port in the entrance hall so that combustion air was drawn into the cold hall and not through the living area. Dirt, chips, and dust from the firewood stayed in the hall, and inside the living area, the enameled tile stove, six to eight feet high, stood clean and warm.

A parallel principle was applied in the *Holland* or *jamb stove* used in this country. This stove, usually made of five cast iron plates and two legs, opened into the fireback of the kitchen fireplace and stood out from the wall in the living room. It was fueled from the kitchen and both cooking fire and stove fire vented up through the kitchen chimney.

The word "stove" once meant only a heated room, a room with a fire. Such rooms, especially kitchens where fires were a constant necessity, were painted plainly in colors that did not show soot or ash. Parlors for occasional use could be decorated more delicately in lighter colors. As early as 1650 they might be heated by a simple six plate box stove because in Massachusetts, bog iron smelters were at work and foundries were casting iron stoves and *firebacks*, asingle plate that forms the rear wall of a fireplace.

Scientific inquiry in the 1700s opened the search for more efficient ways to heat homes. Count Rumford—born Benjamin Thompson in Woburn, Massachusetts—in his varied and brilliant life served King George III of England and the King of Bavaria, investigating a range of problems broad enough for ten good men, such as effecting changes in soldier's rations, *Hausfrau's* kitchens, stockbreeding, transportation, and fireplaces. His work on increasing fireplace efficiency stands today as a text for masons, a model of scientific method, and a service to this country, even though he was a Tory and remained loyal to the

jamb stove

British King through the revolution.

At the same time another Renaissance man was studying an equally diverse span of subjects but he was no Tory. He was patriot, printer, poet, scientist, with, inventor, diplomat, and above all else, a humanist; he was, of course, Benjamin Franklin. He, too, had experimented with obstreperous fireplaces and had formulated cures, but he went further. In a tinkering, mongering, cunning way that would someday be called Yankee he devised an iron stove set away from the wall that was about twice as efficient as the best fireplace. Being separate from wall and chimney, more of its heat was given to the room. Additionally, it incorporated vertical baffles to draw heat from the smoke and flue gases: It was an admirable invention which promised to economize fuel throughout the colonies. Franklin proudly likened it to a brother of the sun itself. Typically, he refused to patent the stove he called the *Pennsylvania Fireplace*, believing that he had profited too much from others' inventions to take profit from his own.

Franklin's Pennsylvania Fireplace has only a distant relationship to the family of stoves we know as *Franklin stoves*. His original design was copied and recopied; his baffles, the placement of his flue, the size and proportions of the fireplace opening, and most of his principles were lost. He should have taken a patent. Even so, the Franklin was more efficient than the fireplace and in its many forms—fitted with legs, doors, windows, eagles, dunce caps and portraits of George Washington—it warmed all thirteen states as it now warms fifty.

Franklin was also intrigued by the idea of a smokeless stove, a fire that consumed its own smoke. The idea had been tried in several ways.

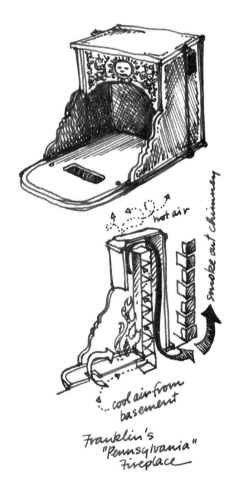

Franklin's "Pennsylvania" Fireplace

Furnus Acapnos

A simple Russian
Fireplace

Franklin reasoned that smoke drawn through the fire and burning coals would be burned clean so he designed a downdraft stove which burned nut coal or small wood on a grate. The outer form was a jar or statue; it was hollow and beneath the grate and ash box it opened into a flue below the floor. It seems to have worked, but like many of his more complex designs, Franklin suggested them for "literary men," since they were most likely to be spending their days near the stoves to write and fiddle with draft and ash and fuel. I can only agree with Dr. Franklin; complicated stoves are wonderful companions for housebound writers.

An earlier attempt at smokeless combustion was the *Furnus Acapnos* shown by French inventor Daveslue in 1682. It was also a downdraft system and the "stem" of its pipe-like shape had to be heated with a brazier to induce the initial draft. Many smokeless stoves have been tried and attempts continue. The next few years ought to see general production of an extremely efficient woodburning stove whose chimney cap will betray no sign of burning beyond a slight shimmer of heat.

Captain Solomon Towne, laying over the winter of 1810-11 in the Russian Port of Revel, was impressed by the qualities of the *grubka*, a Russian brick stove. He had models made and brought them home. Working from the models and directions (which the Ambassador to St. Petersburg, John Quincy Adams, had translated for him) he built many stoves in and around Salem. In New Hampshire at about the same time, brick stoves called *Copenhagens* were being built on the same principle: a brick firechamber burns wood at an extremely high temperature (about 1200°F) due to the reradiant properties of ceramics. Consequently, the wood is consumed almost completely; the hot flue gases enter a set of three to five switchback passages of brick; the switchbacks slow the gas velocity and the brick absorbs so much heat that at the chimney cap, gases are cool. Some claim 90 percent of the heat produced is used to heat the home; 90 percent is probably too high but the surest quality a Russian brick stove has is the enormous mass of masonry that releases its heat evenly over a long period. New interest in these giants is high in New England, some builders reporting a comfortable temperature maintained through the house from one modest charge of wood every twelve hours.

The idea of a stove's heat evened and prolonged by mass is apparent in the *soapstone stoves* of New England. Soapstone (steatite) is a white or greenish talc with a powdery surface that gives it a slippery feel. It is easily cut and shaped and occurs in massive sizes, so it was a natural choice for hearths, ovens, and eventually stoves. Today the dour Vermonters at the Vermont Soapstone Company quarry the pieces and cut the slabs for boot and bed warmers, sinks, griddles and stoves just as they did in the mid-1800s. The wood stoves are fairly simple creatures: top loading in most cases with a side door for laying and lighting the fire and for a draft control. The stone absorbs great amounts of heat and radiates it even after the fire is gone, giving a long, even heat with less tending.

For many families in the 1800s, tending a stove or several stoves was no hardship. Families were large with several boys to chop wood and split kindling. A housewife was what her title implied, wed to the house and bound to its management. Stoves, ornate to a fantastic excess, demanded feeding through the winter and as long

soapstone stove

Victorian Parlor stove

as there was sufficient wood, ox or mule power for hauling, and boy-power to lay it in, each convolution of those grotesquely formal stoves gave heat and kept it as warm as the plainest and most efficient models. There was good trade in *parlor cookers*, decorative parlor stoves with cooking plates under a false top. They may have been for tea or hot chocolate in the afternoon or they might have served summer homes in resort towns which often had no individual kitchens, the family taking their meals at a local hotel; the parlor cooker would have been a convenience for morning coffee or for spring and fall visits when the resort hotels were closed. It is difficult for us to fathom the needs and priorities of our own great-great-grandparents; one can spin conjecture around what is, to us, an odd appliance, a parlor cookstove, or around a set of razors or even a photograph, but the whole taste of the time eludes us. It is gone.

Box stove, 1839

The huge *column stoves*, single and double, must have been overpowering in an already cluttered room, but their columns were functional heat exchangers. Another functional appliance increasing the efficiency of a common stove was the *dumb stove*, a collection of cylinders and boxes soldered or brazed in an air-tight pattern that was nothing more than a flowering of the flue pipe on the second floor, not a stove at all but a heat exchanger to use the warmth of hot smoke, though some were built with small fireboxes to heat on their own as well. *Four o'clock stoves* served the same function; these were little parlor stoves for bedrooms, lit at four o'clock to warm the room by bedtime.

A double column stove with a dumb stove heat exchanger connected above it.

23

Another reason tending fires was taken lightly is that even modest homes often had servants in the 1800s. They stoked and blacked and swept the ashes away from the family's stoves while, belowstairs, there were plenty of homefires going: *laundry stoves* to heat water, stoves to heat pressing irons, and on farms, stoves to incubate eggs, *caldron stoves* to scald hogs, and the farrier's portable *horseshoe forge*. But life belowstairs revolved around the *kitchen range*, a massive expanse of cast iron and brick in a great house, a smaller but no less friendly appliance in a little home. The kitchen range did everything: It cooked fast or slow, it baked, it dried apples and dishtowels and boots, it heated water, it kept salt and crackers, it warmed the kitchen and sheltered the kittens. They came in all sizes, all degrees of complication and decoration, and were able to burn wood or coal.

Fuel could be a problem with any stove. In the winter of 1643 London experienced a shortage of sea coal, coal shipped by sea from the Newcastle pits, and many died of cold. On the great prairies of the American West trees were rare landmarks and pioneers heated with buffalo chips or with one of the improbable hay burners which fed spring-loaded magazines of prairie grass into sensible cookstoves. Even corn ears warmed the prairie winters.

cylinder-feed hay burner

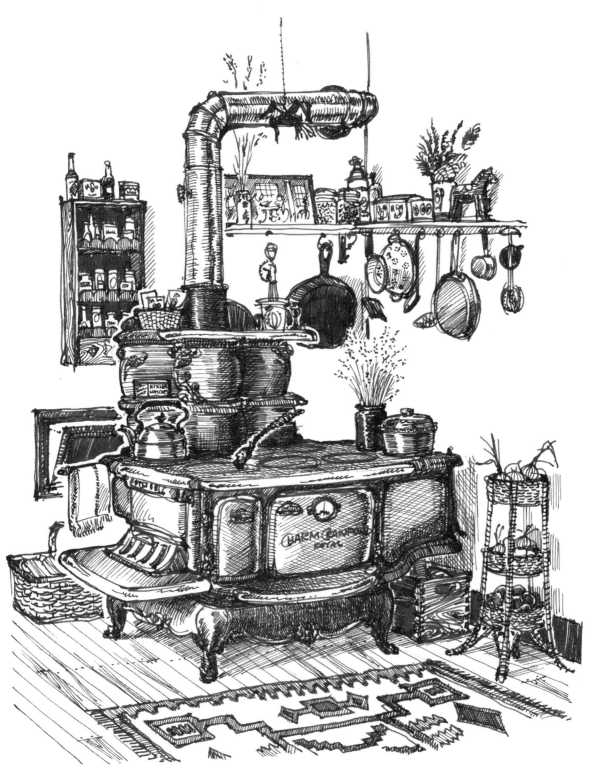

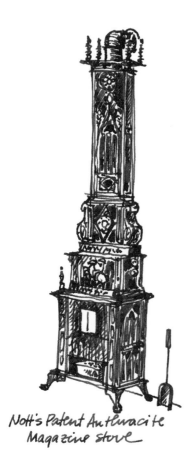

Nott's Patent Anthracite
Magazine stove

an early airtight

Soft bituminous coal was a large part of British export in colonial days. By the early 1800s attempts were being made to use American anthracite coal, harder and more difficult to burn. The Rev. Dr. Euphalet Nott patented a *magazine base burner* in 1820, followed shortly by Jordan L. Mott's *Pyramid Stoves*. These devices carried a large supply of small coal in a vertical magazine over their grates. Air was introduced at the level of the burning grate on one side and the gases from combustion were vented on the other side at the same level. Since the magazine was airtight the burning was confined to the grate where air for combustion swept through. As coal was burned it fell through the grate as ashes and was replaced by unburned coal from above. Once a day clinkers (unburned minerals in the coal) and ashes had to be shaken down with a handle that agitated the grate, making the same rasping roar that coal stoves have made ever since. Nott's stoves suffered in popularity from their complexity, the attendant chances of mismanagement causing explosions, a magazine full of burning coal, and other unpleasantness. Mott's pyramids were easier on the nerves if not as impressive. Base burners of many kinds proliferated, each having its own fanciful design, some with mica windows and nickel-plated hardware. The larger and gaudier models, bright with gleam and windows, stood in splendor on the floors of stores, saloons, lodge-halls and, certainly, barber shops.

The self-feeding coal magazine was one way to stretch the time between tendings. Wood was another problem. The only solution for wood was to burn it more efficiently, gaining all possible heat from every available pound. The early *airtight stoves* were an answer to this need. They were round or oval, sheet steel cylinders, often of the lustrous, Russian steel variety, sitting upright on a cast footed base with a cast top. They could usually be loaded from the top and from a small door at the side. Their sheet steel construction, made uniform and airtight, could be heated quickly and held a fire for a long time because the wood was burning slowly, given only as much oxygen as needed. In short they worked exactly like modern airtights, down to bi-metallic automatic dampers! Their drawback was their thin construction which could burn or rust out in a few years. Some of them though, must have been made of wonderful steel, for they are still to be found here and there, still heating homes with Yankee efficiency.

A Shaker stove with a smoke chamber

Though the Shakers have been regarded with puzzled suspicion, their severe designs and tight craftsmanship are part of our national pride. Some of their pieces are so spare, so lean of purpose, that their look is timeless; they are as contemporary today as they were a hundred years ago. The Shaker stove is a good example. It is an industrial designer's marvel: two castings, base and firebox, three wrought iron legs and one sheet iron door; simplicity, eliminating in a stroke, eight leaking seams. The basic stove, airtight and heavy, is unquestionably efficient and with a smoke chamber above it the Shaker stove rivals any modern woodburner.

As a designer I have always found it exciting that crafts-men and -women devoted so much care and thought and work to the most common things, objects close to the touch, appliances of daily need. The stove has been one of those objects near the body of life and it has enjoyed the inquiry of the great, the skill of the industrious, the art of the gifted, and the devotion of chilly folks for a long, old time.

"Magic Stewart" baseburner

27

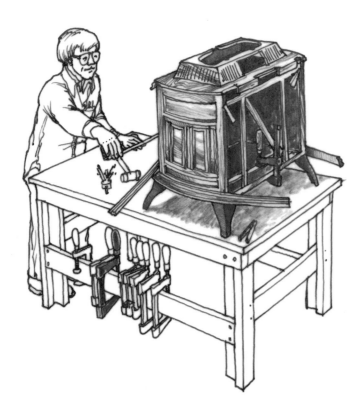

manufacture

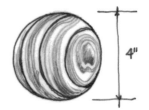

4"

It can take 5000 hours of the patternmaker's exquisitely skillful time to fashion, from first-grade mahogany, the perfectly matching parts of a wooden stove. From these wooden patterns aluminum production patterns are made, thicker by ½'' than the original to allow for a plate as wide and long as the mold *flasks*.

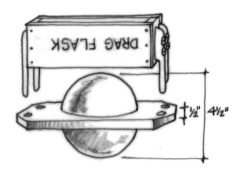

DRAG FLASK

½" 4½"

The production pattern is drilled for placement pins which will hold the *drag flask*, pattern, and *cope flask* in rigid alignment. The drag flask gives the best impression so it will be put down the first and the most carefully. There are two blends of casting sand used here: first, very fine light sand for a precise finish which is sifted on (this is called *riddling*), and then a coarser black sand shoveled over it and *rammed*, packed with tampers or air hammers or even feet (*walking off*) into a shallow box with the drag flask for sides and the pattern as a bottom.

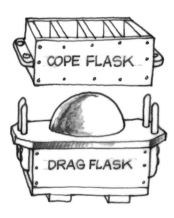

A *bottom board* is clamped on the drag flask and the assembly is turned over. The cope flask, guided by its bushings, settles precisely onto the flask pins and the pattern. *Cope bars* studded with nails span the cope flask; the bars and nails will hold the casting sand in place when the cope flask is lifted.

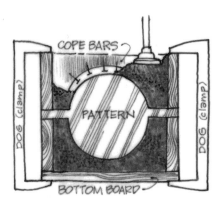

No fine sand is used in the cope flask. This side of the casting will be inside the stove; it will be correct in its dimensions but its texture will be slightly rougher. Black casting sand is rammed in around wooden pins which, when removed, will leave *sprues*— holes to admit the molten iron.

29

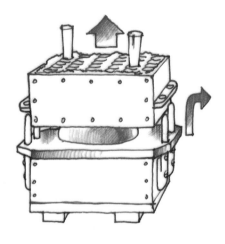

The cope flask is lifted, but not easily: tightly packed with the sand compound it weighs several hundred pounds. The pattern is lifted and removed. Beneath it lies an exact impression of the production pattern in white sand.

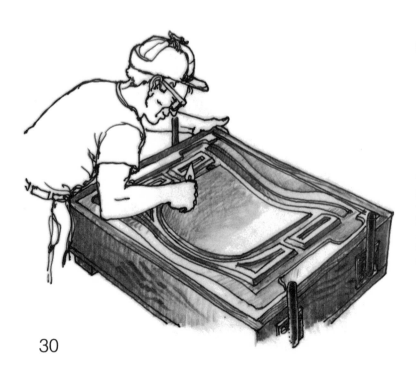

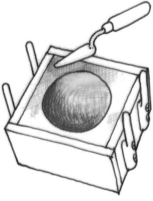

The foundryman examines the impressions, cope and drag. Tiny blemishes and voids can be repaired with his palette knife but the most minor flaw in the impression can ruin the casting; if he discovers a small error in one impression he will reject the entire mold and start over again.

The cope flask is lowered onto the drag flask, registered by the flask pins and clamped together by dogs. Without the pattern and its extra half inch between them a cavity is formed at the center of the mold, the size and shape of the original mahogany pattern to the tolerance of a sand grain. The sprues formed around the wooden pins run into the cavity and/or into *runners*—passages with openings called *gates* that feed the cavity at several places. A tested alloy of molten iron is poured from the furnace into crucibles at 2700° F. Foundrymen strain at the handles and poise the glowing pots at the sprues. They must all pour at the same time. Flame and steam, a smell of heat and metal and charring wood, and

31

the crucibles pour three streams of heavy light into the black sand mold. It is a very old profession, a very old process, changing little over the years. The romans cast their gods this way and the Greeks before them.

After cooling for a time the casting is knocked out of its mold onto a vibrating grate. Sand falls through the grate to be reprocessed and reused. The casting is blasted with steel shot, which scours the surface and removes the last bits of casting sand.

How exact is casting? Each piece is made in a separate mold and is, in minute detail, individual. Since the parts of an "airtight" stove must fit perfectly, considerable hand fitting is done. The runners and gates are knocked off and ground down, the seam at the joining of the flasks is ground flush. Pivots are drilled in doors, drilling and tapping is done to accept bolts. Doors and plates are carefully ground to fit, cooking plates are machined. These parts are a family, now, non-interchangeable. They will stay together in one unique stove.

In final assembly the parts are caulked with refractory cement, gasketed with asbestos rope, and sprayed with heat resistant black paint. Some stoves are kiln fired with a coating of enamel. Packing and shipping are the penultimate steps in the stove's birth: its life begins when it stands uncrated in your home.

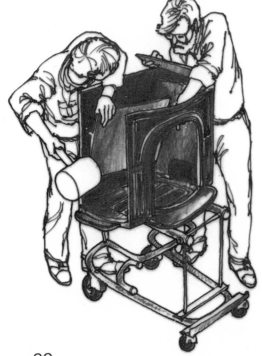

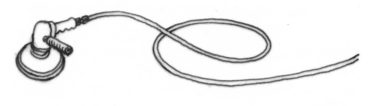

There are few limits to the design of a welded plate steel stove. Any shape can be cut, any seam welded, additions made, ports cut out. The medium is strong and facile. Some makers tout the virtues of cast iron over plate steel; it's an argument best left to our grandchildren, who can say which stoves lasted and which did not. Practically, the heat transmission of plate steel and cast iron are the same. Cast iron tends to be thicker, hence, heavier because of its manufacturing process and the need to retain strength in its more brittle material; the additional weight can even the heat of a burning. Plate steel has internal stresses from its rolling process that may cause it to buckle after much heating and cooling; the buckling should not affect the stoves performance and the welded seams very seldom fail. Some plate stoves are lined with firebrick, which should prevent buckling. It is design which is the prime factor in choosing any stove; the material, cast iron or (heavy) plate steel, is subordinate to the concept.

This is a Sevca stove, welded up from recycled propane tanks.

burning: theory

34

At the end of the bean and pasta aisle in my supermarket is a rack of un-logs. They are wrapped in glossy paper, printed with woodgrain, like the panels on a Chevy station wagon. Shoppers drop them into their carts beside the iceberg lettuce and the enchilada dip. At home they lay them, singly, on their andirons and when they apply one paper match to the red arrow in the middle the whole un-log bursts into technicolor flame for a given amount of time. It's true; I've seen it done. Try that with a two-foot split of hickory.

Alchemical wonders aside, burning wood is a very difficult business. It's a skill. A person who burns wood well takes as much pride in his firecraft as a sailor in his seamanship, and the basis for any skill is knowledge and practice.

You can regard burning in three ways, at three levels: molecular, chemical, and practical. On a molecular level, heat is the measure of molecules' general activity, the speed of their random movements and the frequency of their collisions. A bit of wood is like a gross of blindfolded sparrows in a six-foot cage, flitting aimlessly this way and that, bumping into each other; if you beat the cage with a bat, the level of activity increases dramatically, faster fluttering with more frequent and more violent collisions. The molecules in wood, most of them combinations of carbon, hydrogen and oxygen, bump into each other in random fashion, but without sufficient force to break up the more complex arrangements. When heat is applied, however, the molecules start to jump, colliding with one another violently, breaking complex molecules to form new, simpler combinations. The rebonding itself produces heat, and when the reaction is active enough to sustain itself, the new molecules can bond with oxygen in the air and become a flame.

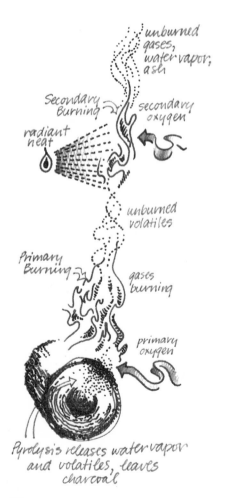

unburned gases, water vapor, ash

Secondary Burning

secondary oxygen

radiant heat

unburned volatiles

Primary Burning

gases burning

primary oxygen

Pyrolysis releases water vapor and volatiles, leaves charcoal

On a chemical level wood is primarily cellulose and lignin, both complex structures of carbon, hydrogen, and oxygen. At about 540°F *pyrolysis* occurs: the breakup of those complexes, producing gases, tars, and charcoal without the presence of oxygen. Oxygen is excluded by the outward pressure of CO_2 and water vapor escaping the heated wood. Because combustion is the bonding of compounds with free oxygen (an *exothermic* reaction, one that produces heat) no combustion is going on. At higher temperatures pyrolysis is almost complete; the escaping gases, hydrogen, carbon monoxide, and methane can ignite (combine with free oxygen) at between 1,000°F and 1,200°F. The gases burn at a temperature of about 2,000°F, producing more heat and hastening pyrolysis deeper in the wood. The charcoal remaining after gases and tars are released will not vaporize (at stove temperatures) and will burn only when oxygen can reach its surface, uninhibited by the outflow of gases and vapors. So there are stages in the life of a fire: heating to drive out water, pyrolysis, the burning of gases and tars, and the burning of charcoal.

On a practical level the well-ordered notions of physicists and chemists are bollixed by the contrary nature of wood. Gas comes to us in a pipe, under pressure, highly volatile, ready to produce a near-perfect flame. Wood comes to us in large, splintery chunks, varying in shape, proportion, and water content. One wood species behaves unlike another, one part of the same tree behaves unlike another. Given, though, a stack of well-cured maple logs, cut and split evenly, your trials have only begun. You cannot hold a match to the log and expect it to politely begin flaming. A match, head down, will sustain its own combustion: it is thin and very dry and given a chemical boost. A log is too thick to sustain its own combustion: volatile gases released must escape the envelope of water vapor and CO_2 driven off by initial pyrolysis; heat produced by that first burning is drawn off into the large mass of the wood itself and into the air; once outside the envelope, volatile gases have lost the heat necessary to ignite. One stick of wood won't do.

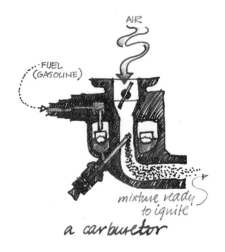

a carburetor

Two logs or more share and build heat. The spaces between them are breeding tracts for combustion. Heat from one log is not dissipated in the air, but beams at its neighbor while it heats in its neighbor's glow. Escaping gases are ignited by heat radiating from both logs. Even the spaces, however, pose some difficulty: with straight, even billets of wood the spaces between logs may be narrow and entirely filled with vapors and volatile gases, creating a positive pressure that excludes oxygen. Combustion can only occur with the proper mix of volatiles and oxygen, this is the purpose of a carburetor in your car's engine. The channels between logs must be narrow enough to concentrate heat and broad enough to admit oxygen; they must be carburetors.

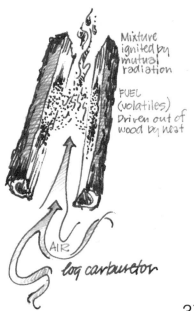

log carburetor

Practically speaking, to start a fire you must arrange to start four fires. You should start on a surface that doesn't draw away heat so cold iron would be bad but an insulative bed of ashes is as good as you can get. The *first* fire is a tinder fire, paper or birch bark or some easily lit material which will burn intensely to support ignition of the *second*, the kindling fire. It is important to give the delicate tinder breathing room, not to let it be crushed and suffocated by the weight of fuel above it; a block of wood, a few pieces of kindling or a half-burned log can hold the logs above the tinder. The kindling is dry and thin, cross laid in a lattice with care for air space and the whole fire should be a well-built structure but loose enough for a mouse to run through. Laying on the logs or splits, really, for the *third* fire requires foresight, a kind of intuition about how they will fall when the kindling burns through.

The *fourth* fire is the continuing fire, adding fuel cleverly and in the right amount. The engineer of a fast steam locomotive was always faced with a quandary: his boiler was hottest at the end of his water supply; he could play out the time of highest efficiency at the risk of exploding his boiler, or he could safely bleed in fresh water, cooling his boiler and reducing pressure. Your quandary is somewhat less drastic: you can gain heat from the last and hottest part of the fire, charcoal pulsing with heat and a dim, blue flame, or you can add fresh wood, cooling the fire for a time but assuring the fourth or continuing fire.

All this is sufficient for building a campfire, but a campfire is not sufficient, at least for heating a home. The best and most successful open fire is a profligate waste of fuel. Air rushes into the base of the fire from all sides, a draft of cold air following it. It feeds the yellow flames and the glaring coals and rises, consumed, as a pillar of wasted

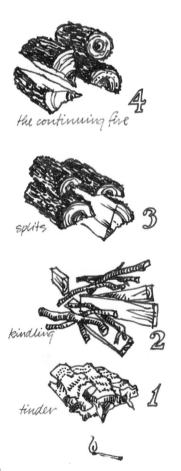

the continuing fire *4*

splits *3*

kindling *2*

tinder *1*

heat. Ten to 30 percent of the flame's energy is expended as radiant heat: some of it given back to the fire itself and some given to those who stand about with their fronts warm by the fire and their backs cooled by the inrush of cold air. A common fireplace may reflect slightly more radiant heat into the room and store some in its masonry, but as temperatures fall the aggregate efficiency falls with it: for every cubic foot of warm, room air the fire consumes and sends up the chimney, a cubic foot of cold air is drawn in from outside.

There are three kinds of heat transfer: *radiation*, the light rays of energy from the flames; *conduction*, the travel of energy through a solid, iron or brick, for instance; and *convection*, the transfer of heat by currents of heated air (or water). A campfire heats by radiation. A fireplace heats by radiation, by minor convective currents of air passing the masonry, and even by conduction of heat through the masonry and into the rooms adjoining the chimney. Primarily, however, fireplace heat is radiant heat. The addition of heating ducts passing around a metal fireback enhance its convective heating abilities to some extent, but the amount of heat escaping up the chimney is still enormous.

The body of the problem is this: to extract the maximum amount of heat from a given amount of fuel, maintaining the draft, minimizing creosote build-up in the flue, lengthening burning time and facilitating maintenance. There are many solutions, each assigning the various parts of the puzzle different weights of importance. In any involved problem a solution that will satisfy all specifications is rare. In this case, on the basis of a fuel that varies over a wide range of characteristics, an ideal solution is hardly possible. There are solutions and half-solutions.

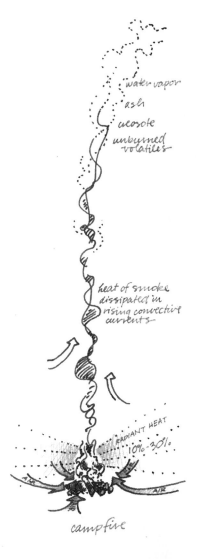

campfire

The stove itself is a beginning. Using the least sophisticated log burner we bring the whole fire out into the room, lift it off the floor, and place it in a conductive container. All this encourages convective currents to begin at the hot stove plates, rise to the ceiling, cool, and fall away from the rising currents toward the edges of the room. The black stove plates also radiate heat. Make no mistake, this simple stove can heat a space very well if given large amounts of wood and attention.

We can increase the efficiency of the stove by extracting heat from the flue gases. Lengthening the stovepipe will give more heat to the room; in old country schoolhouses the stovepipes were hung from rafters across the width of the room and the students were grateful for the extra heat. Fins on the flue pipe will radiate more heat and so will a "stack robber", an arrangement of tubes or fins or passages with a blower to extract heat from the flue gases. These are half solutions; they may do more harm than good and they may occasion some danger.

The gases that leave a stove are hot, varying in temperature with the heat of the fire, the efficiency of the stove, and the loss of heat along the flue. When you are drinking a gin and tonic by the poolside in the summer the humid air meets your cold glass and the water in the air condenses, forming beads of moisture on the glass. Tars and volatiles in the flue gases do the same thing at a higher temperature. When the temperature of the walls of the flue falls below a point of condensation (varying itself, with the makeup of the gases) droplets of tars form. We call this condensate *creosote*. Creosote can be runny if a good deal of water vapor accompanies the smoke, or it can be tacky and gooey but it is always flammable. It is also corrosive, charged with formic, acetic, and other acids. It attacks steel and passes easily through mortar. As it ages, increases, and dries, it changes form, becoming flaky and brittle. There will come a time when a particularly hot fire (classically the Christmas tree and/or wrappings) will light the creosote, and then you have trouble; a violent fire the length of your flue, shaking the stovepipe, turning it red hot, licking through cracks and chinks in the chimney at wood beams and rafters, sending up a gay but dangerous plume of sparks. It is an unpleasant and potentially disastrous calamity. No, reducing flue temperatures with a long stovepipe run or a stack robber is not advisable unless you are a chimney sweep with a lot of spare time.

Another solution to heat extraction is control of the fire. "Airtight" stoves, controlling the amount of the air reaching the fuel, reduce the rate of combustion and the velocity of the stack gases. The fire is not expending all its energy in one high peak, but stretching it out over a period of time. The lower velocity of the gases carries less unburned air up the flue and, of course, draws less cold air in. Combustion in an airtight can, however, can be too restricted; the fire simply smolders, doing little more than pyrolyzing the fuel and sending all the volatiles and tars up the chimney, wasted as fuel and dangerous as creosote.

To avoid creosote in the safest and most efficient way, all the tars and volatile gases must be burned up in the stove. To accomplish this complete reduction two things are necessary: very high heat in the firebox and a supply of oxygen. Firebox heat can be maintained with liners of steel, or a firebrick lining that insulates the firebox from the heat drain of the stove's steel sides giving heat to the room. "But wait," the small woman in

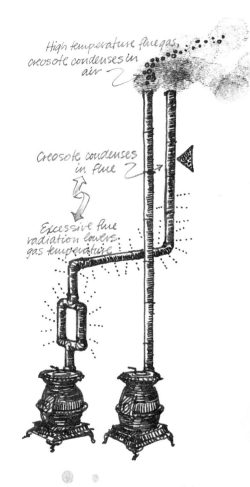

High temperature flue gas, creosote condenses in air

Creosote condenses in flue

Excessive flue radiation lowers gas temperature

41

the back row calls out, "is that not the purpose of the stove? To give heat to the room?" Ah, madam, you are an apt pupil with a sharp ear for discrepancy. Yes, you are right, but we are now attempting to solve that multifaceted problem of wood heat by minimizing the dread creosote. If you will bear with me, it will all be made manifest in the next paragraph. For now, let us pursue the supply of oxygen. Most oxygen serves the pyrolyzing process and gas combustion in and around the fire mass, surrounding the body of fuel with spent gases, CO_2 and water vapor. Some volatile gases do escape, though, and to ignite that supply of gas a fresh supply of oxygen is needed. The air that feeds the fire mass we can call primary air, for it is the first part of a process, primary combustion. The air used to burn the escaped volatiles we can call secondary air, and their burning is secondary combustion. Most airtight stoves provide primary and secondary air supplies, hoping to complete the burning of gases and tars. Under good conditions, with dry fuel in a well designed stove, secondary combustion takes place at times in the cycles of a fire. It is not continuous, but the burning of wood for heat is not a perfectly orderly procedure.

And now, madam, to address your query. Indeed, the purpose of the stove *is* to heat the room, and if the firebox is insulated by liners or firebrick to maximize combustion then heat should be given to the room outside the firebox. And this is another solution: to keep the hot flue gases inside the stove longer. In a simple log burner the flames of combustion lick at the exit flue and hot gases are shunted directly outside to heat the birds—no second combustion, no benefit from the hot smoke. In a sophisticated log burner (what else is a woodstove?) gases from the

diagonal draft in a barrel stove

S-pattern around a baffle in a Cawley-LeMay

updraft through a grill in a pot-bellied stove

shielded, hot firebox are mixed with secondary oxygen and (ideally) burned, then they are led through one or a series of switchbacks that contain the gases longer and allow the stove to give more heat to the room. Stoves designed on the Norwegian model have a horizontal baffle; gases are obliged to travel in an S-pattern, expending heat on the baffle and on the inner surface of the upper chamber. Other stoves have more complex baffles and separate chambers for secondary combustion. Several have an entirely separate smoke chamber above the body of the stove. A few have small blowers that force air through channels around the firebox or around a smoke chamber. This solution adds to efficiency, there is no doubt, but some are too efficient during a large part of a fire cycle and extract so much heat that abundant creosote condenses in the flue which is too cool.

A mechanical solution uses a bimetallic strip attached by a lever or chain to a draft flap. As the temperature of the stove rises with increased combustion one side of the bimetallic strip expands more than the other; this inequity deforms the strip, moving the lever or slackening the chain which, in turn, closes the draft flap. With less draft the fire slows and cools; the bimetallic strip contracts, pushing the lever or tensing the chain; the flap is lifted and with more draft the fire grows hotter to begin the cycle again. This thermostatically controlled draft is a way to flatten the rising and falling curve of the fire's growing and subsiding heat. It sounds very good, and to some degree it works, though it is difficult to say that it works better than simple draft adjustments.

Another way to flatten that curve is to make a heavy stove, a mass of material that heats up slowly and cools slowly. This is the principle of

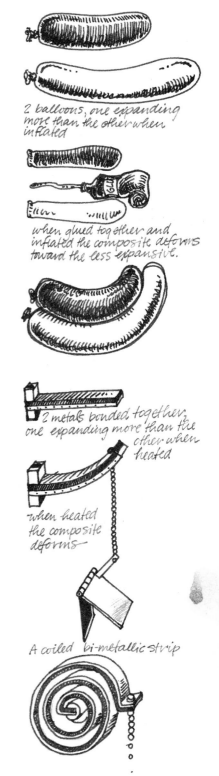

2 balloons, one expanding more than the other when inflated

when glued together and inflated the composite deforms toward the less expansive.

2 metals bonded together, one expanding more than the other when heated

when heated the composite deforms

A coiled bi-metallic strip

43

the soapstone stove and toward the end of the burn it is comforting. At the middle of the burn the heavy stove sheds as much heat as any other stove. But assuring yourself of long-range gains on a frosty morning is a chilly business that takes plenty of character.

Combining and stressing solutions, designers have produced hundreds of stoves, but which is best?

"Well?" Ah, the woman in the back row again. "Which one *is* best?"

Best at what, madam?

"Best at heating a room, of course."

Which room? What is it like, this room?

"Sir, are you being impudent?"

Madam, forgive me, I have no desire to be offensive. I am attempting to make a point, but unfortunately at the expense of your patience, I must admit.

"Very well, then. Let us define the room as eleven feet by twenty feet with a ceiling height of eight feet. I have such a room. What is the best stove for this room."

Where?

"I beg your pardon."

Where is this admirable room? How is it situated in its house? And this house, how is it insulated and how well oriented to the sun? What cover from the wind does it have and what is its latitude?

"I believe I now see your point, sir, but are there no figures to guide the purchaser?"

Yes, of course. Stoves are rated in BTU's (British Thermal Units, a small unit of heat) and in the cubic and square feet they may be expected to heat.

"But you have made it plain that a stove's worth depends on the specific room it warms."

Downdraft in a Tempwood

Around a baffle in the smoke chamber of a Lange

Complex baffling behind the fireback of a Vigilant

I hope so.

"Are you implying that these figures are worthless?"

No, they are very useful as a comparative tool to gauge the output of one stove against another, but they are only relative figures and not, practically speaking, absolutes.

"Then the high claims these manufacturers make may, I infer, be thrown into a cocked hat?"

Madam, I did not underestimate your perception.

"Well, sir, I am displeased. I have come to you for guidance and beyond a few humble conclusions and an airy explanation you do little but discount what indications we do have."

Forgive me.

"What are proper recommendations for a stove?"

At the risk of your further displeasure I will first tell you what are *not* proper recommendations. Claims, no matter how well substantiated, of a stove's fire keeping qualities are not good footing. Any reasonably tight stove can be filled tightly and tuned down to a dark smolder for a long time, but what you are creating is a generator of creosote and creosote is, I promise you, dangerous. A good figure for keeping a burn is eight hours: beyond that you are probably forcing things a bit.

Another shaky source of information is the direct testimonial. All stove owners love their stoves and ascribe almost supernatural virtues to them. Chevy owners love Chevys, Ford owners swear by Fords. A stove is such an intimate family friend that a man who didn't recommend his stove would be a poltroon. Keep your own counsel.

Contemporary Thermo-Control

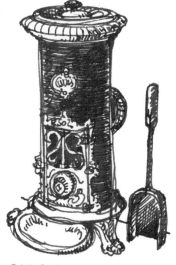

Petit Godin, Contemporary

To select a stove you will have to please your-self and not be marched about by figures. Compare outputs of one stove against another to have an idea of what the heavy duty cabin heaters are and what are sitting room warmers. Decide what you want of your stove. Note that you will almost always err on the side of too much output; buy small. For me, it is important to see the fire of an evening and so I wanted a model that opened into a fireplace. For many, seeing the fire becomes less important as they become accustomed to feeling it.

Some folks will not be satisfied until they can be sure of the last percentage point of efficiency. One mania is as good as another but this quest for efficiency is a paper chase: wood is such a motley fuel that the differences between all the respectable stoves is less than the differences between loadings of wood.

The two most important considerations in buying a stove are beauty and livability. The stove you wrestle into place and install will be a long and faithful companion. Be sure it fits your style. In your concern for an efficient heater do not be guyed into living with a large hunk of industrial iron. Don't buy a stove with a shape that doesn't speak to you. If the graphics on its door don't please you, pass it by. If it looks tinny, it is. Think of the room and house you will heat and buy a stove that fits.

The livability of a stove is its ease of handling, how easy it is to load it, start it, replenish it, adjust it, slow it down for the night and speed it up in the morning. Get an easy stove, with good loading space, clear controls that are easy to adjust. Top loading can be nice, but it's not necessary. An ash apron saves a dirty floor and hot coals from rolling onto the rug.

"Well, young man, you have told us very little

in the way of hard fact. You have in effect, told us that we must make our own decision based on our own perceptions."

In effect, in essence, and in fact, madam.

"Is this not sophistry?"

Perhaps. I would prefer to think it was not. Some years ago I believed that all problems were riddles with an answer, and that a man or woman armed with facts could apply sense and reason in a workmanlike way to rearrange, resolve, and reduce any riddle to an answer. Now I have had the experience of arguing both sides of many questions, of knowing villainous heroes and heroic villains, of seeing evil and expediency and rudeness used as a pry bar to roll aside greater evils. I

Occasionally, your enjoyment of a stove may be marred by a burn resulting from inadvertant contact with a hot metal surface or the imprudent use of a hand as a stoker. Minor burns can be dealt with readily by the stove owner who has presciently stocked his medicine cabinet with a few well-chosen supplies. These include some individually wrapped sterile gauze pads, some gauze rolls 2-3 inches wide, and some first aid spray or cream. Minor burns are those which are no larger than 4-5 inches in diameter and in which the skin surface has neither been blistered nor disrupted by the burn. This generally means that only the most superficial layers of skin have been injured and that complete healing can be anticipated if infection does not occur. The burn should be immersed promptly in cool running water for several minutes. If the injured area is soiled with dirt or ashes, it should be washed gently with soap and water, care being taken not to disturb the surface of the skin. A first aid spray or cream should be applied to the burn (butter, lard and other home remedies don't really help much), following which the burn should be covered with a sterile gauze pad and wrapped loosely with clean gauze. The use of adhesive tape directly on the skin should be avoided, as tape may cause further injury to the burned area. The burn should be inspected daily for signs of infection (increase in redness beyond the original confines of the burn, swelling, or drainage of pus), the appearance of which should prompt a visit to a doctor. It is normal for many burns to peel, much like a sunburn, during the healing phase. Others may form a scab, which will fall off when healing is complete.

One further note: any burn, no matter how small, can be a source of tetanus (lockjaw) for those who are not properly immunized. If you have not had the full complement of tetanus shots in childhood, plus a tetanus booster in the past 10 years, or, if you are uncertain about your tetanus immunization status, you should receive a tetanus booster injection as soon as possible after a burn.

minor burns

Michael A. Lew, M.D.

Styria heater, Contemporary

am older and no wiser, in fact less sure of what wisdom I had salted down before. I am dismayed to tell you that the opportunity to make a hard decision based scrupulously on fact and reason is rare and in human matters, unheard of. When I first understood why a physicist friend consulted the I-Ching about decisions, I lost a part of my reliance on facts; "I can decide about a gear or a material," he said, "but what do I have to go on when I think about my life and what I do with people?" I still believe in reason; logic is the only tool we have, and a lack of reliance is not always a lack of faith, but Bert Bigelow, out of the depth of his heart and catholic experience, quotes me the title of his favorite Goya: "The dream of reason produces monsters." Forgive me for spinning out the thread of an answer into a tapestry, but fire brings out, as I have said, the philosophical side.

"We may only hope that brings out sufficient heat."

Madam, have faith.

burning: practice

A day with your fire is a good lesson. You have a dead fire in the morning and you must build anew. Appraise your mound of ashes; use your shovel or stove hoe to spread your ashes evenly. If you have more than you need to insulate the bot-

Some equipment for home woodburning

49

tom of the stove then shovel some out into the ash bucket or a metal pail (there are always a couple of red coals lurking in the gray). The ashes are fine for lawn or compost pile if you have acid soil. Be sure that air inlets inside are open and un-clogged; they should have a straight shot at the fire and not have to climb over ashes or around burned-out butts.

Lay your fire with skill and deliberation. In a Norwegian type like the Cawley-Lemay, you lay it with tinder and kindling toward the door, because the fire will burn back away from the door. In a cross-draft stove like the Vigilant, you lay tinder and kindling toward the primary air inlet tube on the left. In a Temp-wood you lay the fire upside down: logs on the bottom, smaller splits next up, kindling next, tinder on the top. Once the draft begins the flames and their heat will be blown away from the primary inlet. Every possible bit of

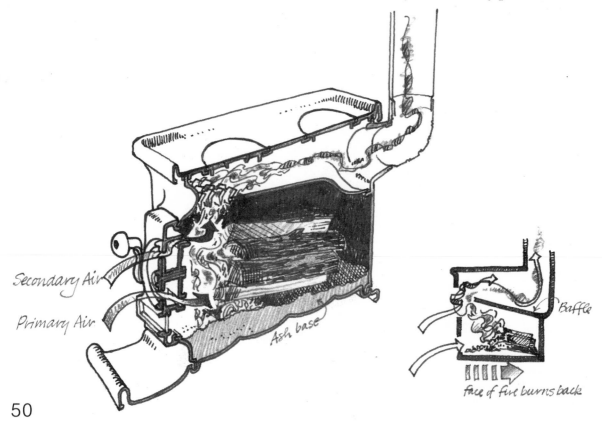

Secondary Air

Primary Air

Ash base

Baffle

face of fire burns back

50

heat should be used to dry and ignite the body of fuel.

The first fire of the day should lay down a good bed of coals for the continuing fire to build on, so your immediate need is a hot, complete fire. If you have dry wood, generous kindling, and enough tinder to light the mass of it, then you are well set. Open the draft controls all the way or, if you have a fireplace/stove, open the doors. A hot, healthy fire, once begun, can be harnessed to your stove's system.

This first fire needs more tending than the continuing fire. The cold stove, cold draft, and cold wood conspire to drain heat and enthusiasm from the blaze. You may reset the splits, re-arrange the kindling coals, or even add more kindling. A pair of leather foundry or fireplace gloves is very useful for the fussing and reworking and, later, for adding splits in just the right place with-out burning your wrists or the backs of your hands. It's good to keep some wood drying beside the stove; really dry wood starts so much easier and the moisture driven out of it helps humidify the house. Too much wood can be a problem, though; with a big pile of logs in your corner you are less likely to notice small forest friends exiting the warmed wood, hungry from a long rest and eager to breakfast on your Chippendale and floor joists.

Now you have a good fire, a hot stove, and a glow of coals. Let it burn down a little. If you have a fireplace stove the doors should be shut and the bypass closed to get the air passages hot. It should be cooking along now, drawing well and putting out heat.

When the first fire has consumed some of itself (let's say half until you get the hang of it) open the bypass, if you have one, and open the stove up to rake coals and fuel toward the inlets—

front or side—as much as seems convenient. You're not running a computer, you're only messing about with a stove. Lay in splits or logs on the fire mass with breathing space between. The purpose here is to weight the fire mass toward the inlets so fire progresses as a controlled face away from the inlets and forms more or less stable draft-flow patterns. This is an ideal; some days the magic works and some days it doesn't. You will have fires along a strata and fires along one side or the other and even fires through the core of the fuel. Remember that wood is a good insulator and adjust accordingly to give your stove optimum heat, but in all probability it will do just fine on its own. Remember that heating with wood is like sailing: it takes thought to keep it on course.

Close it up and go about your business. You can reduce the draft to a lower setting now, but keep a healthy fire. A sickly smolder creosotes your flue and wastes most of the heat value in the fuel by leaving tars and volatiles unburned.

Give a thought to the stove now and again. A good sign that it is toward the end of its burn is the high heat of the charcoal burn. When the fire is reduced to coals and a few chunks of wood you can remake it with fresh fuel, warmed beside the stove. Before you open the stove door, slowly open the draught control all the way and let the flue heat up a moment. This will minimize back-puffing of smoke and even a wisp or two of flame. Rake the coals and lay in the splits and logs, intelligently. Button up again, reduce draft, and return to work.

It's not necessary to wait till the end of the burn to add logs. You can poke a stick of wood in whenever you think about it or you can load it regularly on a loose schedule: breakfast fire, noon fire, dinner fire, night fire. A good stove will leave you alone, though; it will run itself for a long time without any attention. That is one of the chief reasons for having a stove.

Let the fire burn down toward evening, down to angry, red coals. Rake them toward the inlet and make a careful fire of a full load. Give it ten or fifteen minutes of open draft to start it and then reduce draft a little lower than your daytime setting. Not much lower, just a little lower. (Wood-stove buffs are full of brag about the "fire keeping" qualities of their stoves, but their flues are sticky, black and dangerous.) Go to bed comfortable and confident. In the morning you'll have a warm room and coals to begin.

I take pleasure in my early morning trip to the bathroom. I say hello to the dog and make a stiff face at the cat; I tend the fires, push a few coals about and drop on wood; I open the draft so the kids can dress in front of the stove when it's cooking along; I look at the kids sleeping and then I go back to bed and put my arm around my wife. I'm Dad, and that feels good. That's one of the reasons I have a stove.

the wood range

I never had a fireplace nor woodstove before I met the huge iron friend which resides in Clearwater's galley, a Record; New Pioneer. In May of 1977 I became the ship's cook and the woodstove was just one more lesson to be learned in a whirlpool of unfamiliar foods, a limited budget and the guessing game of quantities of food for 15 people. In the beginning even building a fire was an accomplishment. The difficulties were compounded by my own ignorance: as the youngest of four children I had wheedled my way out of chopping wood and learning about the better burning woods.

Because storage space is limited on the sloop, at times we sometimes run out and have to use what is at hand. I remember gathering driftwood near Verplanck on the Hudson River. Later I learned that fresh water driftwood is all right to burn but salt water driftwood causes the inside of a wood burner to rust out. Early November breakfast was once delayed because the green saplings we had woven and shaped to form a bin, then cut up for the galley, took a long time to catch.

Cooking on Clearwater's woodstove was and is a unique experience shared by many. Because I was so inexperienced I survived by delegating a meal to any willing volunteer. The benefits were multifold—we learned from each other. I like to bring wood into the galley a day early to allow it to dry and reach room temperature. The battens used to construct Clearwater's winter cover make excellent kindling and a fast fire. After cleaning out unnecessary ashes, I check to be certain all vents are open. Clearwater's stove has a vent below the fire box, a slide lever for the oven, and a damper on the smoke pipe. Sometimes I will aid the draw of the flue by burning a crumpled sheet of newspaper on top of the stove next to the pipe. This warms it up and encourages the smoke to rise (the galley walls are covered with stainless steel as insurance against the heat). A light cooking oil on a cloth cleans the cooking surface well; the dirt sticks to the oil and can be wiped off.

Often an inexperienced fire builder will find himself lost in smoke. One way to avoid this is to create a flame (cardboard waxed milk cartons ignite rapidly). At times the wind is causing a down draft; rechecking and adjusting the vents corrects the situation. Occasionally if we are really heeling on a port tack, the firebox would be higher than the stove pipe opening because of the position of Clearwater's stove. Again it might smoke. David Peterson, the first mate, suggests the ideal solution: place the firebox in a fore and aft line with the smoke stack.

Until I learned more about control, I generally treated the woodstove like a gas or electric stove. I simply assumed my fire and oven temperature were right. If something wasn't cooking properly on top, I learned to check what was going on in the firebox or to check the position of the vents. For a rapid boil I place the pot directly over the flame. Vegetable soups can be left on the stove and brought to a rolling boil once every 24 hours. Stews with meats should be boiled once every 12 hours. Don Taube prided himself on making coffee in 20 minutes. He used 1'' x 1'' pieces of red or white oak as well as an old fashioned tall coffee pot. Because the sides of the pot slope inward, the water then rolls in upon itself rather than bursting up to escape. If I want a soup to simmer, I let the fire die down and move the pot to a cooler portion of the stove top, generally off the firebox.

I sometimes cooked with a wok on the stove. I lift off one of the stove lids and place the wok directly above the flame. When the oil began to smoke slightly, the vegetables went in. Continuous attention and wood must be added to keep the fire hot. Waffle

irons can be used upon the stove without the electrical housing.

Some say that placing pots directly on the flame does not speed heating time. It *does* blacken the bottom of pots so much that very dark smudges appear whereever the pots are placed. Soaping the outside of clean pots aids cleaning and reduces blackness.

The oven is controlled by a lever: pushed in it blocks the vent to the smokepipe and causes hot air to circulate around the oven box. Some control can be gained by adjusting this lever, as well as maintaining a hot or cool fire. During my first week on board, I made a cake which usually took one hour at 350 F. It was done in 20 minutes. Like the top of the stove, some control is placement: the inner corner next to the firebox is the hottest. I use a thermometer for exact cooking. I also roast a chicken in a sealed brown paper bag, sprinkling water on the bag when it is needed. The bag does the basting.

Clearwater's wood stove is a grand teaching aid. When a group of youngsters visit the galley, we talk about how cooking aboard differs from cooking at home. We discuss what is left from burning wood as

Boomer Peas Salad

1 package of frozen peas (fresh if available)
equal amount of Spanish peanuts
1 tablespoon of mayonnaise
2 tablespoon of sour cream or yogurt
squirt of lemon
garlic fresh and chopped
Worcestershire sauce
salt and pepper

Green Bean & Tamari Salad

(compliments of a 1977 summer volunteer)

Fresh green beans, cooked and cooled
Onions and garlic, chopped, sauteed and cooled
Marinate in ¼ cup oil and ½ cup tamari over night.
Stir frequently.
Serve as a cool salad.

With left over green bean salad—make an omelet.

Divine Decadence (David's Hush Puppies)

2 cups corn meal (unbleached white stone-ground)
1 cup flour
2 large onions diced
2 tablespoons baking powder
1 teaspoon baking soda
1 tablespoon honey
1 tablespoon salt
2 eggs
Milk (add enough until texture is thick, not runny)

Fry in hot oil—it should bubble when a sprinkle of water is added. Put mixture on tablespoon and roll off with the backside of thumb.

Best with fish.

Omelet Easy

1 large cast iron fry pan
Separate 9 eggs
To yolks add cottage cheese, grated cheddar, left over green bean salad, basil

In cast iron slowly cook yolk mixture. Beat whites and fold then into the yolks. As the bottom firms, sprinkle top with grated cheddar and place all inside oven. The whites will fluff up and brown beautifully.

compared with oil or gas. Generally one of the group will know that ashes are good for certain plants and the soil. On their way up the companionway, they meet Charlie Noble*, Clearwater's through-the-cabin-top smoke pipe. The moat of water around the pipe prevents the deck from catching fire and preserves the cast iron pipe fitting. Filling Charlie is a never ending duty.

The most enjoyable thing I have learned about cooking on a wood stove was that anyone can do it. I've seen countless volunteers come into the galley a little unsure, cook upon the stove, and later enjoy the grunts of a well-fed crew. I've also learned how to cool a slow, hot body. A dive into the live waters of the Hudson does wonders. Unfortunately the river is not as clean as it could be but "its getting cleaner every day."

When I was asked to share some ideas about the wood stove other crew members joined my excitement. The following recipes come from David Peterson, first mate, many volunteers, and myself.

* This nautical term was taken from a British admiral whose exacting standards of polish extended even to the galley's smokepipe.

Betty Boomer

Sweet & Sour Lentils

Bring to boil & simmer 20 minutes
3 cups lentils
6 cups water
3 bay leaves
6 boullion cubes (optional)
3 teaspoons sea salt

When lentils are cooked, add & heat
¾ cup pineapple & juice
¾ cup vinegar or lemon
¾ cup honey
3 cloves crushed garlic
⅜ teaspoons cloves
3 onions sauteed
Green pepper, chopped fine
Raisins

Serve over brown rice

A savory sea fantasy by Albert Bigelow

57

installation

When the trucker wheels your new stove through the front door with the veins in his neck bulging and his muscles straining, then you know you've really got something, a hefty piece of physical property, a chunk of the universe. It's big and heavy and very quiet, crated in timber and strapped with steel. When you pay the freight, sign the waybill and watch the truck pull away, you may feel, even in your excitement, a little abandoned. There you stand and there stands the crate, holding a large part of your home's new comfort and interest. It is not like a TV set; you cannot twitch up its little antennae and plug it in and watch the evening news. You cannot set it down and play it like a piano. It must be *installed*.

There is a whole school of labor in that word: *installed*. Most of the pieces that furnish and equip our homes are immediately ready for use. Back them up to a wall and sit on them, lay down on them, get pickles out of them. Very few things are installed. Installing implies the preparation of a site, usually with cutting and building, and mounting something in a fairly permanent way. Your stove demands installation as careful as anything in your home. Having a stove is a responsibility of safety, value, and structural integrity.

Take your time. You got along without your stove to this point and you'll get along for a few days more. Don't jerry-build it into just any place to see it work: it will stay that way for a long time. Be honest with yourself and do ti right, the first time. That's easy advice to give but it's really good advice.

You will need good tools for the job. Use the stove as an excuse to get them; consider them part of the stove's cost. The work is not difficult but it is exacting.

There are two basic problems to overcome: venting the stove through a sound, safe flue and insulating around the stove itself. When you consider the solutions of these problems you cannot think of the stove only chugging along in a docile, normal fashion. It is imperative that you plan for the worst. Murphy's Law holds true here. Plan for stray sparks, rolling logs, chimney fires, breakdowns and failures of all kinds. Some of them will happen. Allow for a red-hot stove and a white-hot flue. Count on showers of sparks and burning logs leaping out of your firebox. Plan for the falling of a ladder against the stovepipe. Be sure that your house will survive a chimney fire. I am not trying to frighten you into doing an unnecessarily fussy job, but only saying that planning otherwise is like planning a long canoe trip and discounting the possibility of rain.

The solutions to all the problems of installation are already worked out for you and mandated by your local building codes. If you call your building inspector or your fire department they will describe the clearances and requirements for woodstoves and they will even suggest materials and methods. Your local code is probably similar to the digest of national code pictured here.

When you are uncrating and assembling your stove keep in mind that it is heavy and if it is cast iron, brittle. If it tips over on a hard surface it

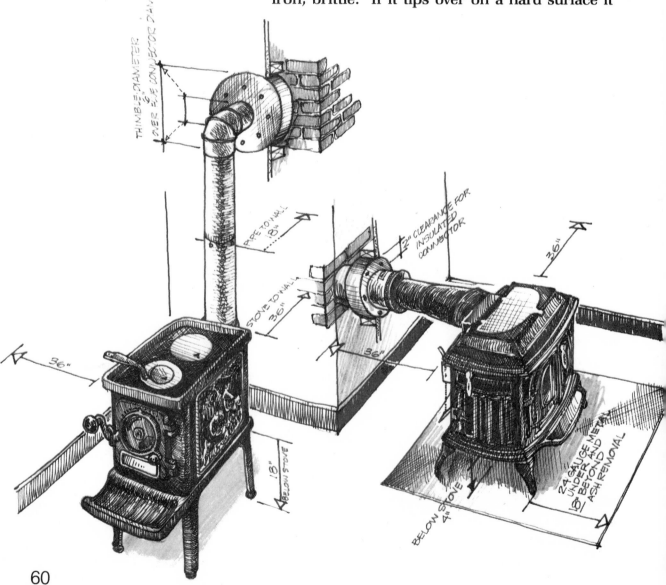

could crack. Lift carefully with your legs and don't strain your back. Get some help to move it into place.

Ralph Waldo Emerson advised a young friend: "In prose you say what you *want* to say. In poetry you say what you *can* say." You put a chair where you want to put it; you put a stove where you *can* put it, that is, where a fireplace or flue is available. The best place is at the center of the house where it can warm all around it. The worst place is on an outside wall, warming a wall that

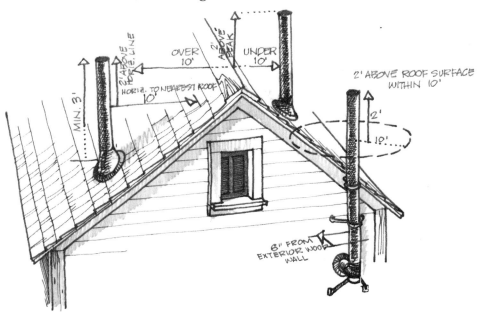

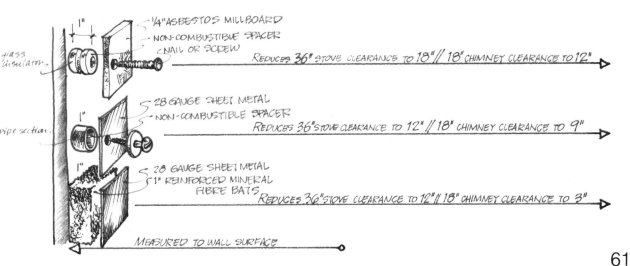

warms the wind. Nevertheless, you may have some latitude and an outside wall may be necessary if you have no workable flue and no straight run to the roof. Do not give yourself latitude by hanging stovepipe across the ceiling of a room. It isn't worth the danger of a whooping stovepipe fire from the condensed creosote. Move the stove about and explore what possibilities you have, because stoves are not easy to relocate once installed.

In thinking of stove placement, turn your house upside down in your mind's eye. See the stove as a spigot of running heat, splashing first on the ceiling below it and starting to fill up the ceiling pan until it runs over the door headers and

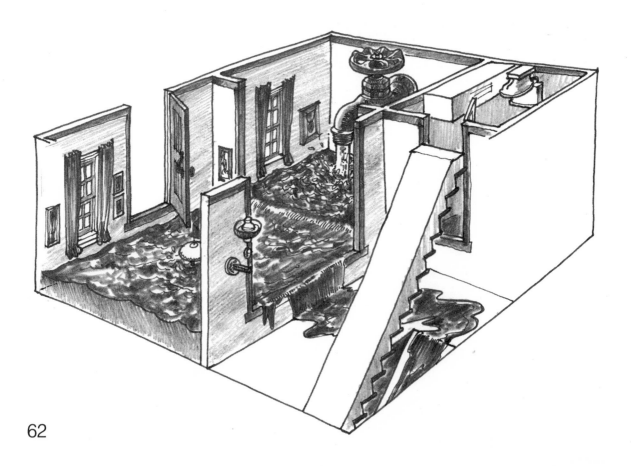

begins to fill up the ceilings of the adjacent rooms or cascades down the ceiling of the stairs and flows nto the second floor. There will be convective currents that run against this upside-down scenario, but the bulk of warm air will stay pooled at the ceiling. Plan a space for a fan—wall, pedestal or table model—to roil those air pools and get them moving around. Consider rooms that can and should be cold. Don't squander heat on closets and cupboards that don't need it. Get it working to warm bodies.

A stove is a pot of fire. Radiant heat beaming from it will bake all combustibles within two yards to a tinder-dry readiness. Floors, rugs, and trim are an obvious concern and they are one reason for a hearth, so a good, expansive hearth extends eighteen inches from the nearest part of the firebox with a good apron for loading wood and catching strays. The hearth is not, however, a sheet of metal or a covering of tile on the floor. Conduction, one of the heat transfers we have not dwelt on, can be a villain around a stove: dark tiles and red tiles collect radiant heat; conduction brings it through floor and subfloor and joists where it can concentrate at seams and corners, waiting for a hot load from the fire to ignite it. The hearth can be firebrick, tile on firebrick, tile on firebrick, tile on asbestos board (*not* asbestos cement board which conducts heat readily), or metal on insulating spacers.

Before you settle on a flue, inspect it and have it inspected. Use a flashlight and a mirror or go ahead and get filthy. Take a *good* look. Is it lined with tile? That's very good. Is it lined with mortar? Not as good. Is it plain brick? Marginal. Is it scaling and missing patches of mortar and generally shabby? Unacceptable.

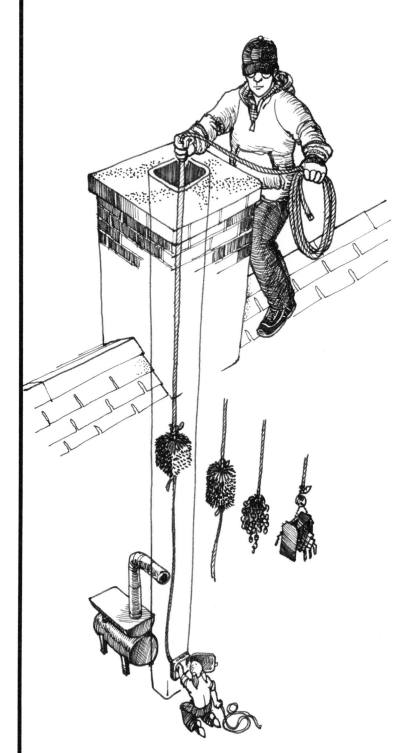

As carefully as you may burn, your flue is going to accumulate a coating of creosote. The very superiority of modern stoves—their air tightness—is their debility, causing a low oxygen smoulder that sends most of the volatiles up the chimney unburned to condense as creosote. At some point in almost every burning your stove will be lining the flue with black goo. This will harden into a brittle plate that can eventually reduce the cross sectional area of the flue. This reduction and the fire hazard creosote poses makes it necessary that you clean you chimney regularly.

Some woodburners have their chimneys cleaned once a year, some after a given number of cords (three or five, whatever seems proper for their stove and style of burning). If you keep your stove booming along with a hot, consuming fire, once a season should be fine. If you insist on closing your stove down to keep over-long fires you will need a cleaning more often.

The best way to a clean chimney is to have it professionally swept. Chimneysweeps are popping out of chimneypots all over the country with the new interest in woodstoves. Generally a sweep will give you an estimate and many feel that a free inspection of your installation is part of their business. You can find sweeps in the yellow pages or in newspaper advertisements.

You can sweep your own chimney, of course. It's high-up wobbly work and if you're not at ease padding around your roof, don't do it. The creosote is not difficult to dislodge and the tools are available: brushes, proprietary tools, and even chimney-cap mounted pullies that can pull cleaning brushes up and down the flue from inside the house. A burlap bag full of chains or a wad of tire chains does an acceptable job, too.

Chimney sweeping is a damned messy chore and your chimneysweep is ready to deal with it. If you are, too, put down plastic or paper all around your cleanout, wear a dust mask, put on old clothes and gloves and get to it, but get to it regularly.

JA

If it is at all questionable, plan to line it with stovepipe or have a contractor rebuild it. Call a contractor in for an estimate and compare his price with the price of a new insulated stack (a little over $1.25 per inch with incidental expenses). Lining with stovepipe, plain or insulated, is workable but lining a chimney with mortar by yourself seems messy and chancy. Creosotes will invade the mortar itself and pass through cracks and chinks in brick to make fuses from your chimney fire to your woodwork. This hard look is the most important part of your installation.

Even if your flue seems fine, ask your fire inspector to look it over. His approval may be mandatory in your area and additionally, it's always good to give the fire department an idea of your home's layout. Your building inspector will give your installation plans his appraisal and many professional chimney sweeps will amake a free inspection. You are not alone.

There is a possibility that a flue will be too large for your stove. It will take time to heat up and a cold flue doesn't encourage draft. You can insert stovepipe or try a constricting chimney cap.

Two heat sources can share a flue if it has sufficient carrying capacity (determined by the height of the chimney and the cross-sectional area). Ask your building inspector about code restrictions and calculations (a table is provided in the *Ashrae Handbook* and the *Woodburner's Encyclopedia*).

If you are planning a new house for wood heat you have an opportunity for the ideal: a masonry chimney at the center of the house, exposed wherever possible, lined with flue tile of the proper capacity. Project your needs for any other heat sources (water heaters, backup furnace,

furnace for resale) and build in separate flues in the chimney. The mass of warm masonry at the core of the home will even your heat and ease your worries. If you are building or installing a stove in a warm climate where the stove will be fired up only in the evenings, opt for a prefabricated insulated chimney: it is small, heats up quickly and so occasions less condensation during start-ups.

You can flue into an existing fireplace in three ways: into a face plate across the opening, into a plate across the throat of the smoke shelf, or into the masonry above the mantly. The first two are dependent on the height of your stove's takeoff (remember to add the height of your hearth). If the takeoff is low enough you can have a sheet metal shop make up a 10 or 12 gauge plate with cups, cut for a round or oval stovepipe, to fit face or throat. Make a stiff cardboard model for them to work from and make sure the model fits.

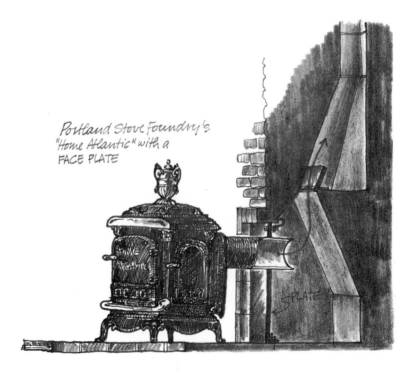

Portland Stove Foundry's
"Home Atlantic" with a
FACE PLATE

Measuring gets muddled, fireplaces are seldom built squarely and it's easier to shave off an eighth inch of cardboard than to file it off 10 gauge steel. Asbestos cement board is hard to cut, cracks spontaneously or with a mismanaged log, and conducts heat. It's a bad choice.

Cutting into a flue is time consuming and difficult. Exposing the flue can be a problem in itself and this is another time when you will need your mind's eye to penetrate the blankness of a wall and surmise what difficulties lie beneath it. Then you will need your good humor to laugh off what is really under the paint. Make your initial incision through surface and plaster and framing to a scribed line the width of your *thimble*. This is the collar that surrounds an insulated metal flue and keeps it at a proper distance (see clearance sketches) from framing and other combustibles. Some folks cut a hole just big enough for an insulated metal section; there are people who enjoy

Vermont Iron Stove Works' "Elm"
with a THROAT PLATE

shark waltzing and Russian roulette, too. The larger thimble diameter will give you some room to work at the masonry, and you'll need it. Ordering the insulated flue, remember that it must project at least four inches from the wall; heat radiates from the uninsulated flue pipe at right angles to its length, but some distance must be

It may take some involved measurements to locate you flue exactly, but take your time and mark it. Mark the position of the studs around it and the nails in the studs, if you can. Try to visualize the structure under the surface.

Scribe the circle for the thimble and cut it out. Remember that there are nails, wiring, and plumbing in the wall. Go carefully.

maintained diagonally.

Wear protective goggles and a dust mask when you start into the brick. Both hand sledge and cold chisel are tempered and when struck they can throw a splinter of steel that will pierce your eyeball. You can help yourself along with a heavy duty drill and a masonry bit, and you may

Cutting brick begins slowly and progresses more rapidly as the opening widens. Wear your goggles against brick chips and steel splinters; you may even want a mask against the brick dust. Work back to your chalk line as closely as you can.

Cut, fit, and fasten headers to the framing above and below the opening to anchor the thimble.

find three sizes of chisel are helpful: one-half, one, and two and one-half inches. Chalk a circle the size of the insulated flue pipe. Work at scoring a single brick, then at the mortar around it, then an scaling it away. It gets easier as the hole becomes larger.

The opening of the insulated flue pipe should be flush with the inside face of the chimney flue. The space between metal and brick should be

Butter the inside edges of the opening in the masonry with refractory cement. Set the flue pipe, its inner opening flush with the inner wall of the chimney. Seal the opening with more refractory cement and screw home the thimble. Attach the flue pipe, crimps *down*, securely with sheet metal screws or with self–drilling/tapping fasteners, right down to the stove.

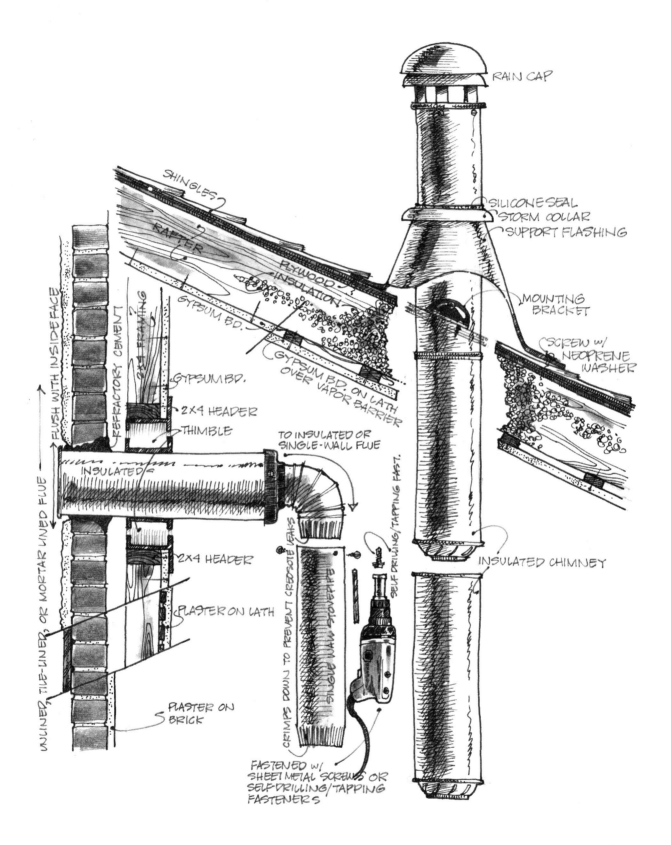

RAIN CAP

SILICONE SEAL
STORM COLLAR
SUPPORT FLASHING

MOUNTING
BRACKET

SCREW w/
NEOPRENE
WASHER

INSULATED CHIMNEY

SHINGLES

RAFTER

PLYWOOD
INSULATION

GYPSUM BD.

GYPSUM BD. ON LATH
OVER VAPOR BARRIER

2X4 FRAMING

FLUSH WITH INSIDE FACE

UNLINED, TILE-LINED, OR MORTAR LINED FLUE

REFRACTORY CEMENT

GYPSUM BD.

2X4 HEADER

THIMBLE

INSULATED

TO INSULATED OR
SINGLE-WALL FLUE

2X4 HEADER

PLASTER ON LATH

PLASTER ON
BRICK

SINGLE WALL STOVEPIPE

CRIMPS DOWN TO PREVENT CREOSOTE LEAKS

SELF DRILLING/TAPPING FAST.

FASTENED w/
SHEET METAL SCREWS OR
SELF-DRILLING/TAPPING
FASTENERS

71

TallBoy

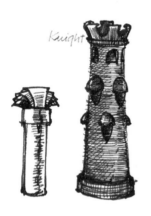

Knight

Leeds 3-ring

filled with refractory cement and the thimble screwed home. If the flue between the through-wall or through-ceiling connection and the stove is not insulated, each section should be fastened to the next with three sheet metal screws. Mount them male side down, even if you must use a double-female piece at the stove; with male ends down any liquid condensed creosote will run toward the stove on the inside and not seep out of every joint and drip on your floor. Creosote stains, sticks, and has a harsh and unseemly odor. It's wretched goo altogether.

You can reduce clearances in one sensible way: hang a metal sheet on insulated spacers behind the stove and between the stovepipe and combustibles. The metal catches the radiant heat and the moving air behind it insulates the wall from the metal. (See the clearance sketches for details.)

Chimney caps are more than whimsical decorations, but they are decorative and some are whimsical as well. If your home is under the brow of a hill or in the lee of high trees, without caps currents of wind can toot down into your chimney and cause backpressure from the wind. Rain can also get in and combine with creosote to form a corrosive, smelly mess. So, caps are often a good idea.

These sketches should help you plan a sound, safe system—hearth, stove, stovepipe, through-wall connector, chimney flue and perhaps even a chimney cap. Woodstoves are only dangerous if they are installed by impatient, careless people who do not recognize danger in its bud form.

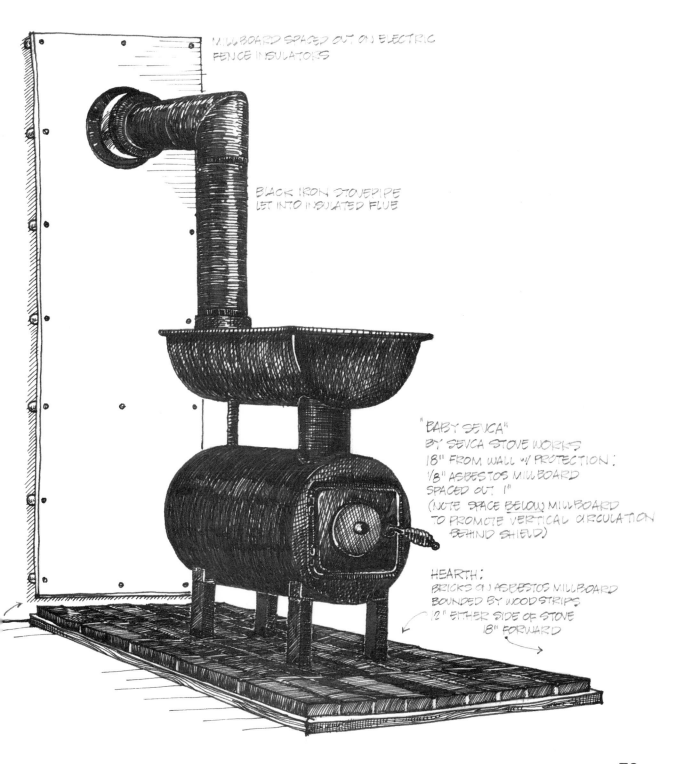

MILLBOARD SPACED OUT ON ELECTRIC
FENCE INSULATORS

BLACK IRON STOVEPIPE
LET INTO INSULATED FLUE

"BABY SEVCA"
BY SEVCA STOVE WORKS
18" FROM WALL w/ PROTECTION:
1/8" ASBESTOS MILLBOARD
SPACED OUT 1"
(NOTE SPACE BELOW MILLBOARD
TO PROMOTE VERTICAL CIRCULATION
BEHIND SHIELD)

HEARTH:
BRICKS ON ASBESTOS MILLBOARD
BOUNDED BY WOOD STRIPS
12" EITHER SIDE OF STOVE
18" FORWARD

73

wood

If this book were to persuade every reader in North America to heat with wood, it would be a failure as an argument, and an environmental disaster. Successful, this book would function like a vacuum tube, encouraging and accelerating tuned impulses, discouraging and even repelling off-key impulses.

Wood heat is not for everyone. Grant that most of the world relies on wood for cooking and heating, but make the reservation that this is a country of clustered population, agglomerated in cities. Universal wood heat would lay a thick shroud of smoke over all the centers of population; particulate matter in the air would react with sunlight to hang moving palls of smog over the landscape; ash would collect on cornices, dust clothes hung out to dry, and collect as dirt on kids' wrists and ankles; green belts around cities would disappear as supermufflered chainsaws with worklights appeared; the chainsaw carnage would fill emergency rooms; as wood prices rose, so would the energy costs of shipping wood to consumers from the receding forest line. Not a single production woodstove today could pass EPA emission standards. Add to that the probable environmental impact of more extensive logging and you have a simple fact: wood heat cannot be a mass movement.

Is it then, elitist? Yes, in the sense that anything you reserve for yourself and deny others is elitist. Almost everything fun or meaningful is elitist: I do not want every hiker in America crushing the ferns around my favorite trails and no trucker wants a pompous windbag like me on his citizens band channel. It is elitist because it is a pleasure only a few out of many can share and it is not elitist because it is a labor and a responsibility only a few out of many are equipped to bear.

Heating with wood is for responsible people in tree-bearing country who enjoy the labor and accept the inconvenience of it, who enjoy the control over their own comfort and the ties it affords with the real cycle of things.

The first immigrants to this continent settled on the thin coast of a dense forest a thousand miles deep that forbade crops and herds, concealed bears and catamounts and the original tenants, and swallowed up runaway shoats in thirty feet. A family with a thousand acres of forest was poor; a family with thirty acres of cleared ground was wealthy. The forest was an enemy stronger and more feared than Mohawk raiders. Yet it was a generous enemy, yielding heat and light and wares of wood that made life possible: spoons, chairs, barrels, doors, piggins, firkins, ladles, combs, hayforks, fences, troughs, bowls, and bedsteads. By 1800 the East was logged out. Forests were gone and more land stood open to cultivation than sees the sun today. The stone walls that march through dark woods of third growth timber today bounded open fields when King George III took snuff at Windsor. Second growth stands are now a rarity and virgin timber a national treasure in the East. They laid down the forests and used the timber, and they were only a small fraction of our number today.

China and Japan, once forests, eventually had to adapt to a reduced supply of wood in every part of their life. Even their cuisine responded: small morsels cut to cook quickly in round-bottomed pans that concentrate heat—the most cooking from the least fuel.

Today in our culture wood is all around us. It serves us in four major capacities: as a building material it is the fabric of almost all private housing, concrete forms, furniture, floor and trim; as paper it is the medium of communication for business, literature, news, and for you and I at this moment; it is a basis for chemicals of astounding variety, for alcohols, dyes, and resins; it is, last and presently least, a source of heat. It can be said that many stands of timber are underused and, consequently, undermanaged, but no one who has seen

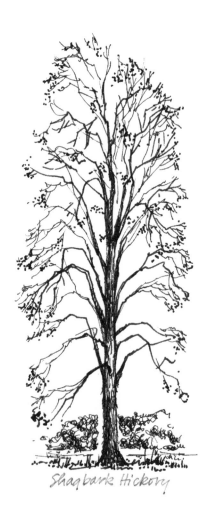

Shagbark Hickory

a forest disappear before the well-managed saws and tracked machines of a logging company can be totally comfortable with total management. Wood *is* a renewable resource, but the scar of a commercial logging operation is painful and a long time healing. When the forest returns, in twenty years, it's not the same forest; it's a homogenized, vitamin enriched, "white bread" woods of select fast-growth conifers in which no catamount or Mohawk raiding party would be comfortable.

It might be as prissy for a woodburner to flinch at logging out a stand of timber as for an eater of hamburgers to be disgusted by a meat packing plant. But this is the very point: most of us are carnivores, but we are not all woodburners. There should be as many woodburners as can save a significant amount of fossil fuel energy and as few woodburners as can gently and appropriately harvest forest without erasing them. Those who can, should, but we are speaking of ideals.

Are there alternatives to oil, gas, *and* wood? Yes, we have coal, which can be bought reasonably, handled neatly, and burned cleanly. In the matter of coal we can look to Britain. The British Isles are far more densely populated than this continent and they have no timberlands. Their oil shortage is more critical than ours and so they are falling back on their geology. Britain has enormous deposits of coal. Their mining operations have been stepped up and their electric railway program brings coal to power plants with the electricity the coal produces. Coal burned in mass can be controlled and its effluents reduced. Processes have also been developed in Britain to change the nature of coal burned for home heating. Sold under proprietary names, processed coal is a clean and practical fuel which has

Sugar Maple

recently been franchised in this country with the U.S. Carbonization Corporation. Manufacturers of many woodstoves, among them the makers of the very efficient Vigilant and Defiant, have developed coal models. The Petit Godin and the Chappee, imported by Bow & Arrow Imports, are designed for coal burning. Lange and Jotul and others market coal stoves. If you live in a city or in an area far from forests, coal can be a less expensive, more convenient, more efficient, and less energy-intensive heating fuel.

Let us assume, from this point on, that you are conscientious, energetic, and you live beside a mixed forest. I don't know why I ever doubted you; forgive me.

You can harvest wood or you can buy it. You may well do both. Harvesting wood, you take what you can get. Buying wood, you can be a little pickier and a little more specific about type and quantity.

What kind of wood is best? Within a few percentage points all wood has the same heat value *per unit of weight*. Density, though, there's the rub. Different woods have different densities; they weigh considerably more or less *per unit of volume*, and wood is sold by volume. Burning characteristics of wood differ considerably—ease of lighting, length of burning, spark spitting, production of coals, etc. But a pound of any wood contains about the same amount of heat, because all woods have essentially the same chemical structure. A preference is usually given to deciduous trees (the "hardwoods" like elm or oak or ash) over the coniferous trees ("softwoods" or "evergreens" like pines or hemlocks or firs) because the hardwoods burn longer and produce better coals and because the resinous conifers tend to throw off more creosote. Woodcutters

American Elm

seldom sell softwoods as anything but kindling, for which it is excellent, easily lit and quickly self-sustaining with a brief but hot flame. Between hardwoods and softwoods density tells the tale: a cord of softwood weight about 2,000 pounds, a cord of hardwood about 4,000 pounds; that is an additional ton of material at 8,600 BTUs per pound.

Paper Birch   Red Oak   Beech

To buy wood you must have an acquaintance with the term *cord*, a singularly anthropometric measure for woodcutting. A standard cord of wood is the amount that will stack four feet deep, four feet high, and eight feet long. The longest log you want to manhandle in the woods is about four feet; that's for width. It's a great effort to stack heavy logs much higher than four feet, and that's for height. As for length, an honest day's work for one man with hand tools comes to about eight feet of four foot logs, stacked four feet high. "How tightly stacked?" asks a familiar voice from the back row. Technically the four by four by eight foot dimensions enclose 128 cubic feet, and a good cord is expected to comprise about 80 cubic feet. Practically, it is yarned that a cord of wood should be loose enough to let a squirrel scamper through but stop the cat that's chasing it. Variations on the cord are played out semantically and mathematically. A dealer might speak of a "face cord," a "long cord," a "short cord," a "stove cord," or a "unit," but these terms have no set dimensions. Demand a price based on a standard cord and calculate from your own measurements: wood in standard cords equals height in feet multiplied by the width in feet multiplied by the length of stack in feet divided by 128 cu ft. It's really the only sensible way to make comparisons. In fairness to the woodcutter, he regards a cord as a measured stack of green four foot logs. As it cures and dries that cord will lose between 800 and 1,400 pounds of water (varying with species) and about eight percent of its volume. If he works it up into stove length billets the saw kerfs will eat up more volume. The cord is an inconsistent, faulty, unwieldy measurement but eminently and even charmingly human.

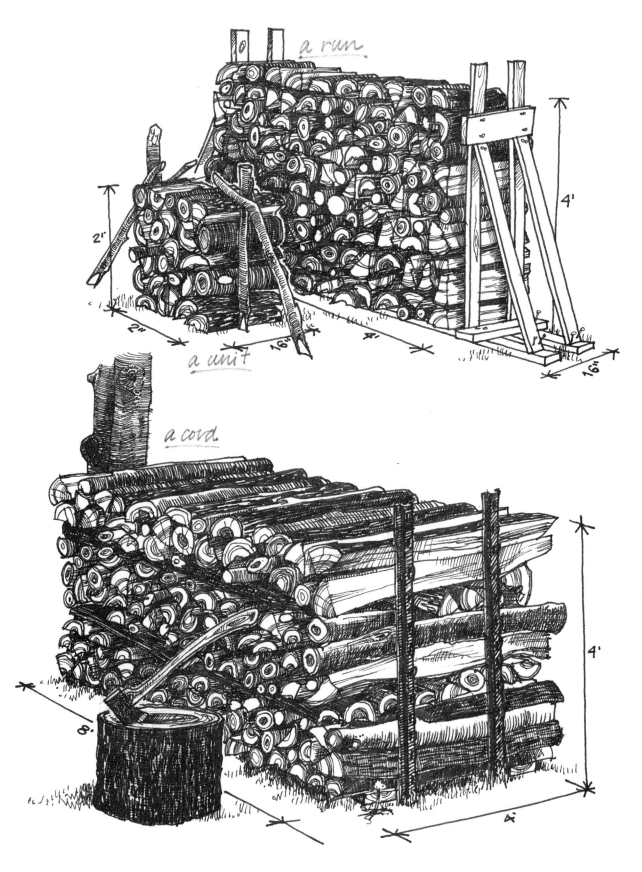

a run

a unit

a cord

2'

4'

2"

16"

4'

16"

8'

4'

4'

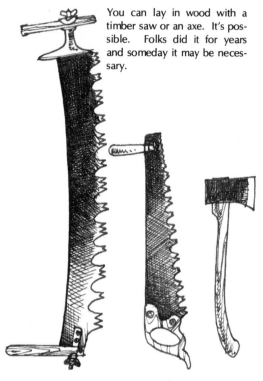

You can lay in wood with a timber saw or an axe. It's possible. Folks did it for years and someday it may be necessary.

This cutter is wearing a hard hat, hearing protectors, safety goggles, snug gloves, and steel-toed boots. His pants are tucked in and he's not wearing any loose clothing to catch in twigs or chains. He is more confident because he feels more secure and is not dazed by the chain saw's argumentative whine. He will make fewer mistakes and not tire as quickly as a cutter wearing only sneakers, a pair of stagged pants, and authentic lumberjack suspenders.

If you buy all or part of your wood, use your imagination. Sawmills discard trimmings; box, skid, and crate factories have scrap heaps; cabinet shops and boatyards are also kindling sources.

If you are cutting your own firewood you have a single imperative: keep yourself whole. Any cordwood or oil bill is not worth an accident with a chainsaw, and chainsaws do not produce minor accidents. Axes are almost as bad, unpredictably striking back at the most skillful woodsman. Even a bucksaw or a "Swedish Fiddle" can give you a nasty remembrance. Fear is a healthy human defense and very honorable between you and the chainsaw because it has the edge on you. Take all the precautions you can think of and adhere to the single most important safety rule: *Never cut alone.* It's all very burly to think of yourself as the lone lumberjack, leading the strenuous life in the Great North Woods, but if you

Buy the best chainsaw you can with any sensible safety option, devour its owner's manual, and pamper it. Attend to its chain tension, its lubrication, its air filter, its spark plug, and its roller nose (if it has one) more than once a day. You've got to *maintain* it in order. The chain running out at the bottom and entering at the top will pull away on an under-bar cut and push back on an over-bar cut.

You can compensate for the cuts and control them but the upper quadrant of the nose is dangerous territory: the bar is whipping around the nose and will kick the saw up and back in a violent spasm. This is the reason for a kick-back guard and chain brake. Learn to cut with the safe bar positions.

are hurt you'll stay in the Great North Woods. Never cut alone.

Eye protection, with goggles or a face shield, is not only sight-protective but spares you an awful lot of blinking and dust-in-the-eye distraction that can make a chainsaw or axe more dangerous. Chainsaws can work up to about 110 decibels and that's seriously loud. If you don't want to listen to music any more or pay much attention to conversation, don't bother with ear plugs (about 60¢) or sound muffs ($8-$13). Snug gloves give you a better grip on saws and logs. Box-toed or steel-toed boots can't help your dancing style but they might preserve it. Some folks with an aversion to branches striking their heads, wear a hard hat when cutting under limbs ($6-$10). If this sounds like overdressing for the part, you're wrong. A woodstove is a way to get a little comfort out of life and it shouldn't be an excuse to hurt yourself.

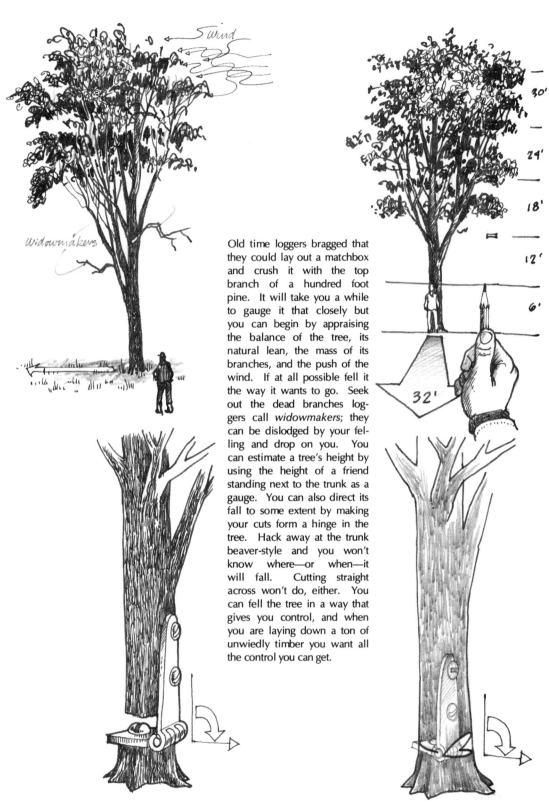

Old time loggers bragged that they could lay out a matchbox and crush it with the top branch of a hundred foot pine. It will take you a while to gauge it that closely but you can begin by appraising the balance of the tree, its natural lean, the mass of its branches, and the push of the wind. If at all possible fell it the way it wants to go. Seek out the dead branches loggers call *widowmakers*; they can be dislodged by your felling and drop on you. You can estimate a tree's height by using the height of a friend standing next to the trunk as a gauge. You can also direct its fall to some extent by making your cuts form a hinge in the tree. Hack away at the trunk beaver-style and you won't know where—or when—it will fall. Cutting straight across won't do, either. You can fell the tree in a way that gives you control, and when you are laying down a ton of unwiedly timber you want all the control you can get.

The first cut is the *undercut*, horizontal and at right angles to the direction of the fall. This cut forms the pivot of the hinge and should be made with care. Some saws have guide lines to sight across for this cut.

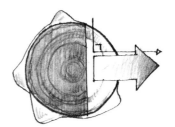

The *face cut* is the next. This removes a wedge of food that would otherwise hold the tree up on that side. It takes practice to make these cuts perfectly, but as you learn remember that undershooting the face cut is better than over-shooting.

The last cut is the *back cut*, made slightly down and parallel to the undercut, directed to meet the face cut an inch above the undercut but stopping short to leave an even thickness of hinge wood. This saw may begin to bind as you reach the middle and a plastic or aluminum wedge (which will not harm the blade) may be necessary to open the saw kerf.

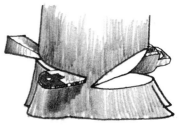

Before you begin any cut, lay out an escape route, clear it of brush and obstructions. The tree may be rotten within or may be split or weakened by termites; it could fall at any moment. You must know your way out. When it begins to go, move quickly but deliberately from the tree at about 45° from the line of fall.

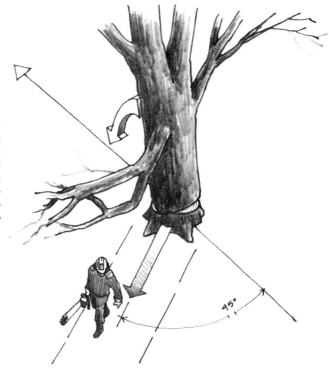

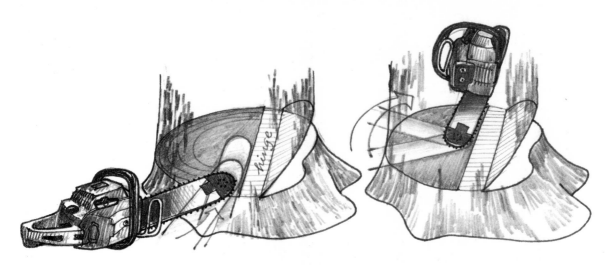

To fell a tree thicker than your bar length you make the undercut and face cut from both sides of the tree. Start the backcut with a *stab cut* begun at the side and behind the hinge with the *lower* quadrant of the bar's nose. Continue inward, pointing the nose directly toward the heart of the tree by degrees. When the cut reaches the center, swing the saw around through the backcut and make your exit from the—hopefully—falling tree.

Standing directly behind falling trees is a risky pastime: they can split vertically, begin to fall, and shear toward the rear.

How much wood are you going to need cutting and/or buying? Heating an average home of two floors, seven or eight rooms, with average air leaks and some insulation, a rough projection would go to five cords for a fall, winter and spring in New England. This is so rough, based on a few specific homes, that it is only conjecture. If you can overbuy you'll be saving money, burning wood bought at the previous year's price and dried an additional year. You can make a more accurate projection by totaling your fuel con-

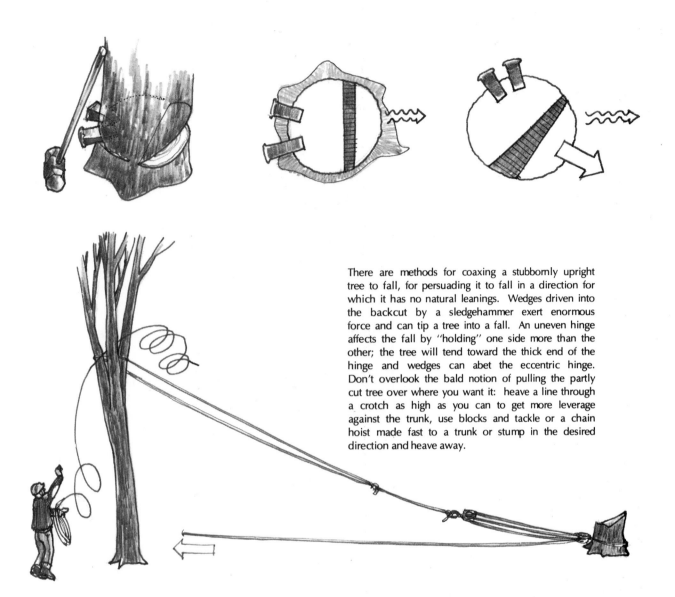

There are methods for coaxing a stubbornly upright tree to fall, for persuading it to fall in a direction for which it has no natural leanings. Wedges driven into the backcut by a sledgehammer exert enormous force and can tip a tree into a fall. An uneven hinge affects the fall by "holding" one side more than the other; the tree will tend toward the thick end of the hinge and wedges can abet the eccentric hinge. Don't overlook the bald notion of pulling the partly cut tree over where you want it: heave a line through a crotch as high as you can to get more leverage against the trunk, use blocks and tackle or a chain hoist made fast to a trunk or stump in the desired direction and heave away.

sumption for the last year, matching it with oil/gas/electric equivalents in the table of woods, and run it through the equation below. The efficiency of your oil or gas burner can be tested by your dealer in a few minutes (or you can test them yourself, see the Time-Life *Heating & Cooling Book*, pp 30-31). Though this looks sufficiently scientific to project wood needs down to the last popsicle stick, it is still a rough guess. You can save some chainsaw work in the woods by doing some maintenance in the house: insulating,

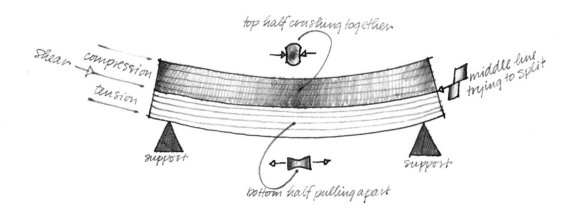

weather-stripping, tightening up all around.

If you don't have a woodlot, someone does. A farmer with whom you can share cut wood, a bog owner who wants his access roads kept clear, a logging operation that leaves tops and limbs in the woods, a developer who is tearing the hateful things out to make room for concrete. You can call your agricultural co-op extension or state conservation department to lease limited logging rights on federal lands for a few dollars; it's a fine opportunity not only to log out some good wood but also to work under the direction of a professional forester and see how a woodlot is managed.

In your own woods, management is a matter

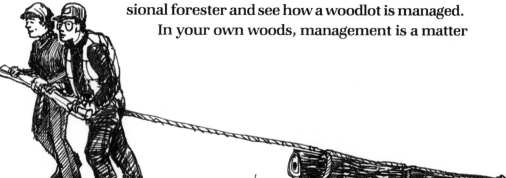

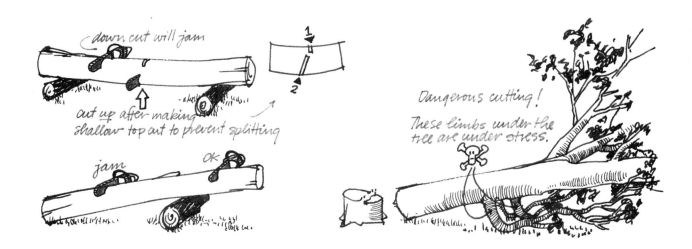

down cut will jam

cut up after making shallow top cut to prevent splitting

jam   OK

Dangerous cutting! These limbs under the tree are under stress.

of good judgement in nurturing the fittest, straightest trees by harvesting the dead, the gnarled, the overshadowed and the doomed. Trees whose canopies spread over healthy neighbors can be culled, and crowded groups can be thinned. A vigorous, tended woodlot can sustain a yield of half a cord of wood per year, and thoughtful harvesting will improve it each year.

The most difficult part of logging seems to be transportation. Getting cut wood out of the forest and next to the door is a long haul. Twitching is the traditional teamwork between woodsman and horse; leaving limbs in the forest, the horse drags out the straight trunk, root first and lengthwise.

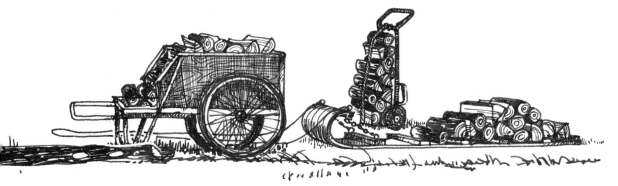

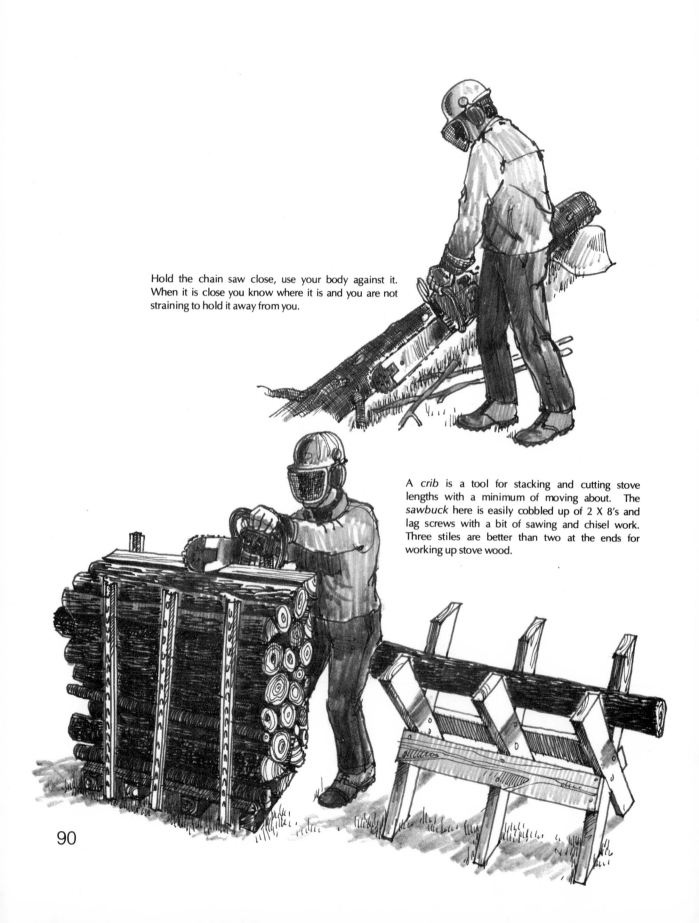

Hold the chain saw close, use your body against it. When it is close you know where it is and you are not straining to hold it away from you.

A *crib* is a tool for stacking and cutting stove lengths with a minimum of moving about. The *sawbuck* here is easily cobbled up of 2 X 8's and lag screws with a bit of sawing and chisel work. Three stiles are better than two at the ends for working up stove wood.

The height of this chopping block is about 20″. The file is handy—to—keep axe, splitting maul and wedges sharp. The hand maul is handy to place and seat the wedges before using the large maul on them, and is also good for tapping the stuck wedges free. The woodchopper is bringing the axe down with an easy heft, letting its blade and weight do the work for him, not straining. He flexes his knees so the blade strikes the billet when the handle is horizontal; if the axe glances off for any reason it will stop in the chopping block and not in the dirt or in a shin.

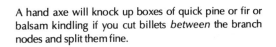

Wood wants to split along center lines of trunk and branches and you want to take its path of least resistance.

A hand axe will knock up boxes of quick pine or fir or balsam kindling if you cut billets *between* the branch nodes and split them fine.

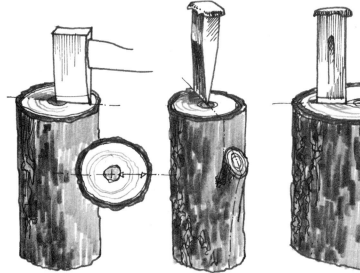

Two loggers can twitch out a small tree hitched to a bar between them. If you live close by your woodlot the best choice is a *Garden Way Cart*; its big wide-spaced wheels make it stable and easy rolling for moving wood and everything else around your spread. A normal wheelbarrow has a small wheel that does not move well over roots and rocks, sinks into spongy forest soil, and is tippy on even ground. In the snow a toboggan or a wide-runner sled brings out the timber.

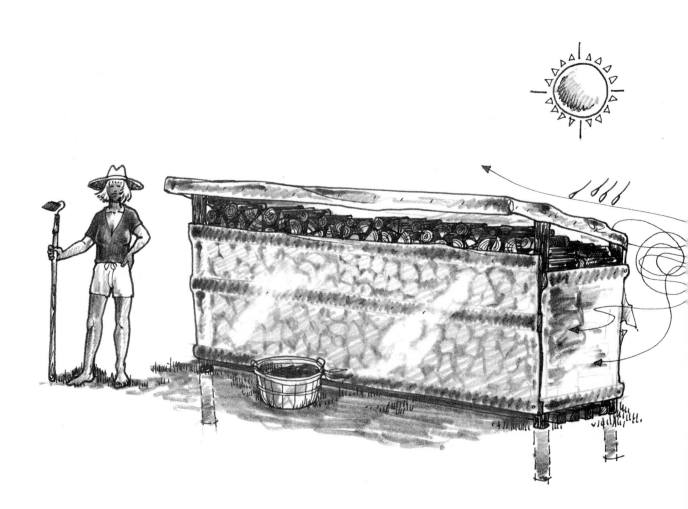

Wood must cure. Woodsmen in the old stove days cut it in the winter before the spring run of sap. They laid it where it was felled, in trunks or four foot logs, up on blocking to lose some of its water. After mud time they could bring out the now lighter wood to "work it up."

Working up stove wood takes a piece of time. You begin with four foot logs and end with splits of stove length. Cutting to length and splitting speeds the release of moisture, so you may well be working at next winter's wood this spring and through the summer. Some woods folk work up stove wood with a splitting axe (a heavy axe with a quick taper), some with a splitting maul and wedges, some with s slide-mounted wedge and a sledge, and folks with a lot ful of logs use powered splitters. When you use a splitting maul or a sledge on wedges, put on your goggles or face shield. Splitting is a pleasant, satisfying chore that works up a sweat and stretches your muscles. It's a solitary chore that allows time for reflection, a good job when you're thinking something out.

The best wood is dry wood. How dry your wood will be depends on how you store it. Stored outside its moisture content may wither to 14-25 percent. Under cover without heat it can dip to 10-15 percent and in the heated house, 5-12 percent. Curing usually takes more than a year, but wood stacked in the sun under a vented clear plastic shelter can be ready for good burning in three to four months. Storing wood in the house or garage could be disappointing; trees are homes for a nation of wood eating insects that think of a frame house as dessert. A woodshed, even a simple structure, will shelter and cure stovewood almost as well.

Woodburning is a skill and truly, it begins with the wood. The woodburner comes to know the forest and its families of trees, becomes a woodsperson who sustains and nurtures the whole health of the forest. An experienced woodburner stacks his woodpile like a pantry, filing species for needs: a bin of kindling here, pine for a quick fire there, a load of fragrant apple for special evenings, a section of hickory for long winter nights, rows of hard, dry oak. The woodswoman sharpening her splitting axe, the woodsman cleaning his chainsaw, the family around the stove—for them heating has become something more than a switch to turn on, their comfort comes from the forest and their labor and their new won knowledge.

wood, some relative characteristics

WOOD	HEAT VALUE/ CORD	COAL	OIL	GAS	SPLITTING	COALS	COMMENTS
Apple	24×10⁶ BTU	1.09	245	300	= = =	+ + +	Fragrant
Ash, white	20.5	.93	209	256	= =	+ + +	Best to burn if you must burn unseasoned wood
Aspen, quaking	12.5	.57	128	156	=	+	
Beech	20.9	.96	213	261	= = =	+ + +	
Birch:							
sweet	22.5	1.02	230	281			
yellow	21	.95	214	263	= =	+ + +	Will rot unless split and dried
paper	18.8	.85	192	235			
white	18.5	.84	188	231			
Cottonwood	15	.68	153	188			
Chestnut	15.6	.71	159	195			
Elm, American	17.7	.80	181	221	= = = =	+ + + +	
Hickory, shagbark	24.7	1.12	252	308	= =	+ + + + +	
Locust, black	23.8	1.08	243	298			
Maple:							
red	18.6	.86	190	233	= =	+ + + +	
silver	17.9	.81	183	224			
sugar	21.3	.97	217	266	= = =	+ + + +	
Oak:							
red	21.3	.97	217	266	= =	+ + + +	
white	22.3	1.05	235	288	= = =	+ +	
Sycamore	16.8	.76	171	210			
Tamarack	14.9	.67	152	186	=	+ +	
Walnut	18.9	.86	193	236			Why burn a walnut?
Willow	13.5	.61	138	169	= =	+ +	
Yellow Poplar	12.5	.57	128	156			
	millions of BTU's	tons	gallons	cubic feet	= easily split = = = = = = = = = difficult	+ few coals + + + + + + + + + many	

95

the babysitter

Heating with wood has at least one problem which is not, at first, obvious: the babysitter. The babysitter is usually young and has no experience with fires, is often accident-prone, and requires special instruction.

How can you prepare the babysitter for an evening in your home? One approach, the most sensible for most teenagers, is to turn on your oil furnace, let the stoves go out, and spend a carefree evening. But for young people who take an interest in stoves and seem more, let us say, imaginative than most, you may very well decide to leave a cheerful blaze in welcome.

In an ideal world the flues have been recently cleaned, there is a stack of dry wood beside each stove, a pair of insulated gloves hangs handy-by, and a fire extinguisher is mounted within reach. Because it is not an ideal world, the fire department's phone number—and yours if you're not far away that evening—are on the pad by the telephone.

You should take the time for a short, serious talk with your sitter before you go out the door. Consider the effect on your stove and flue of an over-conscientious loading. Chimney fires wait for an occasion to start: built-up creosote doesn't ignite with your program of steadily conservative fires. A hot fire could provide the occasion. Without alarming your trusty replacement you might mention this possibility, instructing him or her to recognise the symptoms of a chimney fire: roaring draft, crackling in the flue, followed by the creaking of expanding joints and a shower of sparks issuing from the chimney-top.

The only piece of advice that applies to every chimney fire is to close all air intake ports at once. That done, the best plan is to call the fire department.

The fire department is called for many chimney fires and often arrives after the excitement is over. Our local fire chief tells me he uses a weighted chain in the chimney to remove any unburned soot and checks the roof rafters, floor joists, and other woodwork abutting the chimney for signs of spreading fire. If the fire is still roaring he believes in waiting it out and almost never sees a need for ruining ceilings and walls with water.

As you get to know your stove you will probably develop a daily schedule for fuel loadings. You ought to be able to tell another person quite accurately when and how much to add. This will keep the sitter's fire in line with those you've been burning night after night, making it less likely to push up the mercury in your absence.

If your babysitter is greeted by a crackling fire slowly cooking the family's stew, you can go out certain that they will be well cared-for. A good stove is a good provider.

Dorcas Adkins

97

other homefires

"You have given a great deal of effort to cautious encouragement, sir and I am like to admit that the prospect you portray is rosy and warm."

Thank you, madam.

"But the bald fact is that fire is fire. These stoves seem well designed to keep it in check and I accept the necessity of them."

Hardly a necessity this early in the game, madam.

"I will even venture that their physical comforts outweigh the uncomfortable closeness of the raging flame."

You overstate your case.

"Less insolence and more humility for your own theatrics, sir."

Touche!

"I, for one, will always have a watchful eye to detect the first wisp of trouble, and I sincerely hope that I must abide no further open flames in the home."

Your vigilance is wise and admirable. You will have no major difficulties because of it, and in time your suspicion will reduce itself for want of feeding to simple caution, but as for your dislike of flame, madam, you deny yourself many pleasures. We are drawn to the flame like moths to a candle.

Breakstone Lantern

99

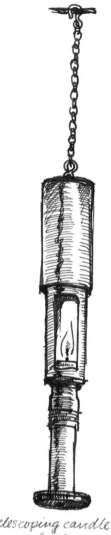

telescoping candle
holder

Svea 123R

Take the candle itself. There is a spell to the pulsing flicker of a taper that flatters, enhances. The face of a lover or a joint of beef or the clarity of a wine benefit. It is intimate light. I recall evenings in a tent in Canada when the canvas seemed to quiver with the light from one candle in a dented Breakstone lantern inherited from my grandfather. Its sides were rumpled like an old gray suit and its mica windows were crazed and it was the only light for fifty miles.

Later, in another tent, there was a telescoping candle holder with a spring-loaded cylinder that pushed a stearic acid candle up as it burned at the end so the flame stayed steady inside its glass ring. Just outside the flap of that tent a Svea 123 stove hissed at night and in the mornings, making small meals in small, featherweight billies. They were simple meals and sometimes there were eggs hard-boiling at the bottom of the stews, but they were seasoned with hunger and they were delicious. Other traveling stoves: a pump-up, hot as hell Coleman that was big and heavy for packing, but fast and had a hoarse little roar that was loud enough to keep you company; in the bicycle panniers, an elegantly minimal alcohol burner with an almost invisible, almost inaudible flame that took a while longer but sat in a machined pedestal that looked so Swiss.

And boat stoves! A Tiny Tot on *Pendragon* heated up and dried out the early spring and late fall cabin with charcoal, and it made that little ketch a home when we brought her north in the early May. Rain on the skylight in New York City was an entertainment when it was burning. It was grand to come back to the dock from the city and see the wisp of smoke from her Charlie Noble, and once in the morning, after I had stoked it, I pushed open the hatch and looked out on the river to see a fiery finger write "God is coming," and then "7:15." I was worried; I knew it was about that time, but when the fog lifted it was only the neon finger on the Jehovah's Witness building. The woodstove aboard the *Clearwater* was a monster when it was 104°F in Newburgh, but a few days later it was raining and the monster felt good and we had it smelling like grandma's heaven when we baked bread for which we had ground our own flour, and we only burned one end a little because we were laughing and yarning in the main cabin. The alcohol stove on *Walrus* makes it a home, gives it a supper-on-time respectability which cold sandwiches don't. That regularity, the sense of completeness, is important on a small boat.

Sea Swing stove

Shipmate Ship's stove

101

smoke bell

gimbaled ship's lamp

Aladdin mantle lamp

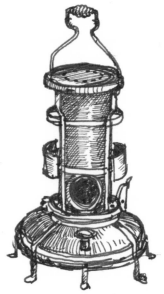

Aladdin heater

On a big boat it's just important to eat well; *Nor'Easter*'s propane galley stove was just as good as any apartment stove but conditions vary; between New York and Bermuda, Dorcas and Dick had to chase a corned beef all over the gally floor, slipping on the grease while *Nor'Easter* rolled in the seaway, and we could hear them laughing on the bridge.

Saving the batteries on a boat or lighting a home when the lines are down, a kerosene lamp is a sturdy little soul of flame. A home without flat wick hurricane lamps is rare along the coast. The tube wick oil lamps are beautiful, a circle of white light in the slim shaft of their chimney. Sally Bulford rented the old cottage on Widows Cove; it was lost for years until someone, a hunter I think, saw a corner in the brush and Mary Churchill remembered that her grandfather had it built as a hunting lodge; Mary had it cut out of the brush and it was just fine; she had the good taste to leave it without electricity and the mantle lamps would whisper under the stuffed ram's heads at night, their glass eyes would gleam; we all loved that place.

An Aga cooker in

The little flame of a fondue pot is a center to gather around; eating together from a common pot is friendly and Bohemian. The little flame under a samovar is different: it is reflected in the polished grace of the urn as it sits at the sideboard, a witness to cordial conversation. Blazing fig pudding is a festive center that calls for songs and cheer, and almost as festive but more intimate, *crepes suzette*.

chafing dish

The big gustatory celebrations always have fire. Pull on your boots and stomp on down to a Texas barbecue to see a whole steer clad in brown, pungent sauce, revolving above an open bonfire. Surf into a luau pig roast on a black volcanic beach and help dig the pit, gather wood, light the fire to heat the rocks, then witness the almost macabre interment of the late porker surrounded by a pagan mantle of fruits and tubers. But the resurrection!

In late summer the beaches of New England are pocked and blackened here and there by clambakes. They are less pagan than pig roasts or barbecues; they have a good nature of their own though somewhat subdued, for in New England the clambake's bonfire is met with quiet appreciation—no one dances about it, there are no chants. Later, when hot rocks, seaweed and flats of food are covered with old canvas sails and awnings, there may be a school song or two, but these canny Yankees save their strength for what's to come: clams, lobsters, quahogs, sausages, frankfurters, Maine potatoes, sweet potatoes, bread dressing, fish filets in brown paper, onions, ears of corn, brown bread and beer. They know what they're doing.

No madam, we still need the flames to light our tinder in us. We cluster around our charcoal grilles as closely as cavemen clustered around their fires in the rocks. The fire is an old friend, and we remember.

106

access

This list is by no means complete. It does not propose to be an encyclopaedic array of every woodburning device here and abroad. There are wide and notable gaps; I have not seen, for instance, a really suitable barrel stove kit, certainly not a kit with a whit of art or whimsey. I would have liked to list axes and chainsaws (my own and favorite is a Husqvarna 340 CB). I am sure to receive reams of angry stationery from hordes of tic-ed off manufacturers, all wondering why I didn't list their stove or Genuine Alabama Grease-Wood or Sure-Grasp fireplace tongs: I neglect all of you out of sorrowful and abject ignorance; be charitable. I would have liked to add a critical bibliography, too, and failing that I can at least mention a few books that will deepen your wood-stove interest: *Fire On the Hearth* by Josephine H. Peirce, out of print and rare but a formidable history; *Stove Book* by Jo Reid and John Peck (pb, $5.95, St. Martin's Press, 175 5th Ave., NYC, 10010), rich color photographs of astonishingly beautiful stoves and their surroundings, a gemlike book; *The Woodburner's Encyclopedia* (pb, $6.95, Vermont Crossroads Press, Box 333, Waitsfield, VT, 05673) by Dr. Jay Shelton and Andrew Shapiro, a work of facts and numbers, a standard reference; *Antique Woodstoves* by Will & Jane Curtis (pb, $4.95, Cobblesmith, Rt 1, Ashville, ME, 04607) indifferent photos of nifty antique stoves; the package of Husqvarna chain saw technique manuals available for $1.00 from Jesse F. White, Inc., (Rt. 16, Uxbridge, Mendon, MS, 01756.

photo by Brassai, "Picasso, 1939", courtesy of the Worcester Art Museum

Abundant Life Farm
P.O. Box 63
Lochmere, NH 03252
(603) 524-0891
heating stoves

Agaheat Appliances
P.O. Box No 30
Ketley, Telford
England TF11BR

AGA's American Supplier:
Russel C. Tarr
14 Hathaway Ave.
Beverly, MA 01915
(617) 927-1235
high quality enamelled cookstoves. Available in coal or oil-burning models.

The beautiful Aga Cooker, Model CB: coal or oil, enamel finish in several colors; 19th C technology in 20th C design.

Aglow Heat X-Changer
P.O. Box 10427
Eugene, OR 97401
(503) 343-7605
fireplace accessories

ALH, Inc.
P.O. Box 7235
Nashville, TN 37210
Aladdin Lamps

Albright Welding Co.
Rte. 15 Box 108
Jeffersonville, VT 05464
(802) 644-2987
Woodsplitters

All Nighter Stove Works, Inc.
80 Commerce St.
Glastonbury, CT. 06033
"Moe" heating stoves

American Stovalator
Rte. 7
Arlington, VT 05250
fireplace accessories

American Way
Dept. 10-OG
190 Range Road
Wilton, CT 06897
fireplace accessories

Amherst Welding, Inc.
330 Harkness Rd.
Amherst, MA 01002
fireplace accessories

Arizona Forest Supply
Box 188
Flagstaff, AZ 86002
AFS Fireplace

Ashley Products Division
Martin Industries
Box 730
Sheffield, AL 35660
(205) 767-0330
heating stoves

Ashley Spark Distributors, Inc.
710 N.W. 14th Ave.
Portland, OR 97209

Jiffy Log Lifter: C&D Marketing

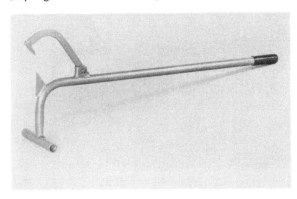

"Moe" by All-Nighter Stove Works: Firebrick lined, with convective air tubes through the firebox, three sizes.

DeDietrich AL-77 wood burner

Atlanta Stove Works, Inc.
Box 5254
Atlanta, GA 30307

Atlantic Clarion Stove Co.
Brewer, ME 04412

Autocrat Corp.
New Athens, IL 62264
(618) 475-2121
cookstoves, heating stoves, circulating heaters

Auto Hoe, Inc.
Box 121
De Pere, WI 54115
fireplace tools

Bahia Bar-B-Que
P.O. Box 1806
St. Paul, MN 55111

Bellway Manufacturing
Grafton, VT 05146
(802) 843-2432
furnaces and boilers

Besta Heater Ovens
Box 887
Charlestown, NH 03603

Birmingham Stove and Range
P.O. Box 2647
Birmingham, AL 35202
(205) 322-0371

Black's
58 Main St.
Brunswick, ME 04011

Blazing Showers
P.O. Box 327
Point Arena, CA 95468
hot water heaters

Boston Stove Co.
Dept. CJ1
155 John St.
Reading, MA 01867
fireplace accessories

Bow and Arrow Stove Co.
14 Arrow St.
Cambridge, MA 02138
(617) 492-1411
one of the wellsprings of the new interest in
woodburning—a broad selection of excellent stoves
& equipment—kind and knowledgeable people, good
service.

The Burning Log
Box 438
Lebanon, N.H. 03766
De Dietrich Wood Heaters, cookstoves, and furnaces

Canaqua Co.
Box 6
High Falls, NY 12440
(914) 687-7457
1908 Baker St.
San Francisco, CA 94115
(415) 346-0752
high temperature sealants and gaskets

DeDietrich #3753 coal burner

Carlson Mechanical Contr's, Inc.
Box 242
Prentice, WI 54556
(715) 564-2481 or (715) 428-3481
Furnaces and Boilers

C & D Distributors, Inc.
Box 766
Old Saybrook, CT 06475
Better'n Ben's heating stoves, chimney cleaners, log splitting equipment

Cawley/LeMay Stove Co. Inc.
27 N. Washington St.
Boyertown, PA 19512
(215) 367-2643
heating stoves in two models, beautiful and efficient design, decorated in woodland animal relief

Cawley-LeMay #600: The larger C/L, convenient counter top height, generously designed, beautifully made, baffled firebox with window, large ash apron. Log length 24-27''.

Chim-A-Lator
8824 Wentworth Ave., So.
Minneapolis, MN 55420
(612) 884-7274
fireplace accessories

Chimney Heat-Reclaimer Corp.
Dept. Y 53 Railroad Ave.
Southington, CT 06489
(203) 628-4738 (ext. Y)
heat reclaimers

Comforter
Box 175
Lochmere, NH 03252
heating stoves

Country Craftsmen
Box 3333
Santa Rosa, CA 95402
barrel conversion kit

Country Stove and Shelter
Paul W. Ramsey
The Exchange Building
Farmington Ave.
Farmington, CT 06032
heating stoves and accessories

Waldo G. Cumings
Fall Road
East Lebanon, ME 04027
(207) 457-1219

Custom Wrought Products
Greentown, PA 18426
Fireplace equipment

Dampney Company
85 Paris St.
Everett, MA 02149
(617) 389-2805
silicone stove coating

Sam Daniels Co.
Box 868
Montpelier, VT 05602
(802) 223-2801
furnaces and boilers

Dawson Mfg. Co.
Box 2024
Enfield, CT 06082

Cawley-LeMay #400: Is not as long as the 600 but just as pleasingly proportioned, log length 16-19". Cooking rack available for both models.

Duravent Insulated Flue sections

Charles Dedrick, Inc.
Stone Ridge, NY 12484

Deforge Industries
P.O. Box 216
Winooski, VT 05404
fireplace accessories

Didier Mfg. Co.
1652 Phillips Ave.
Racine, WI 53403
(414) 634-6633

Double Star
c/o Whole Earth Access Co.
2466 Shattuck Ave.
Berkely, CA 94704
(415) 848-0510
heating stoves, free-standing fireplaces

Dover Corp.
Peerless Div.
P.O. Box 2015
Louisville, KY 40201

Dover Stove Company
Main St.
Sangerville, ME 04479

Dura-Vent Corporation
P.O. Box 1280
2525 El Camino Real
Redwood City, CA 94064
a high quality insulated stovepipe

114

Dyna Corp.
2540 Industry Way
Lynwood, CA 90262

Dynamite Wood Stoves
R.D. 3
Montpelier, VT 05602
heating stoves, furnaces and boilers

Eagle Industries, Inc.
P.O. Box 67
Madison, OH 44057
fireplace accessories

Jiffy Wood Splitter: available from C&D Marketing

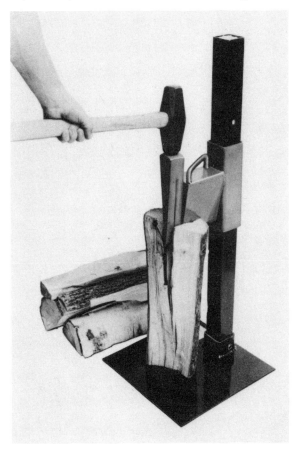

Edison Stove Works
P.O. Box 493
469 Raritan Center,
Edison, NJ 08817
(201) 225-3848
heating stoves

Empire Stove and Furnace Co.
Albany, NY 12207

Energy Associates
P.O. Box 524
Old Saybrook, CT 06475
woodcutting aids

Enwell Corp.
750 Careswell St.
Marshfield, MA 02050
(617) 837-0638
furnaces

Efel Kamina: Belgian combination fireplace/airtight with a glass door.

Jiffy Chimney Cleaner: C&D Marketing

Todd Evans, Inc.
110 Cooper St.
Babylon, NY 11702

Fabsons Engineering
P.O. Box F-11
Leominster, MA 01453

Fireplaces (N.S. Limited)
Suite 215 Duke St. Tower
Halifax, Nova Scotia, B3J1N9

Fire-View Distributors
P.O. Box 370
Rogue River, OR 97537
(503) 582-3351
glass window wood heating stoves

Fisher Stoves, Inc.
504 So. Main St.
Concord, NH 03301
(603) 224-5091
heating stoves

Fisk Stove
Tobey Farm
Box 935
Dennis, MA 02638
(617) 385-2171
barrel stoves

Forest Fuels, Inc.
7 Main St.
Keene, NH 03431
(603) 357-3311
wood/gas burner system

Franklin Fireplaces
1100 Waterway Blvd.
Indianapolis, IN 46202

Fuego Heating Systems
P.O. Box 666
Brewer, ME 04412
(207) 989-5757

Futura Stove Works
Main St. Box 14
La Farge, WI 54639
wood splitters

Garden Way Research
P.O. Box 26
Charlotte, VT 05445
(802) 425-2137
heating stoves
fireplace accessories
wood splitters

L.W. Gay Stove Works, Inc.
Marlboro, VT 05344
(802) 257-0180
heating stoves

Gemco
404 Main St.
Marlborough, NH 03455

General Products Corp.
150 Ardale St.
West Haven, CT 06516
fireplace accessories

The Elm, Vermont Iron Stove Works: A simple, attractive design, well-made, with a plate steel barrel body, cast ends and baffle, and a Pyrex window. Firebrick lined, available with cooktop and matching tools.

Morso #1125 combination fireplace/airtight: unmistakeably Scandinavian in design.

Nashua Doubleheat with forced air convection channels around the firebox.

Glo-Fire
Spring and Summer Streets
Lake Elsinore, CA 92330
(714) 674-3144

Golden Enterprise
P.O. Box 422
Windsor, VT 05089
fireplace accessories

Greenbriar Products, Inc.
Box 473
Spring Green, WI 53588
free-standing fireplaces

HDI Importers
Schoolhouse Farm
Etna, NH 03750
(603) 643-3771

Heathdelle Sales Associates, Inc.
Rt. 3
Meredith, NH 03253
"Nashua" heating stoves

Heatilator
Box 409
Mount Pleasant, IA 52641
(319) 385-9211
pre-fabricated fireplaces

Heat Reclaimation Division
939 Chicopee St.
G.P.O. Box 366
Chicopee, MA 01021
(413) 536-1311
heat reclaimers

Heritage Fireplace Equipment Co.
1874 Englewood Ave.
Akron, OH 44312
(216) 798-9840

M.B. Hills, Inc.
Belfast, ME 04915
(207) 338-4120
furnaces

Hinckley, Foundry and Marine
13 Water St.
Newmarket, NH 03857
heating stoves and stove accessories, excellent and efficient Shaker stove reproductions

Home and Harvest, Inc.
2517 Glen Burnie Drive
Greensboro, NC 27406
cookstoves

Home Fireplaces
Markham Ontario L3R 1GE
(416) 495-1650
971 Powell Ave.
Winnipeg, Manitoba R3H OH4
(204) 774-3834
Morso Canadian Importer cookstoves, heating stoves,
circulating heaters, free-standing fireplaces, fireplace
accessories

Morso 1Bo: This is the slightly larger of two almost identical
models. Takes 22" logs, also available without heat exchanger.

119

Household Woodsplitters
P.O. Box 143
Jeffersonville, VT 05464
(802) 644-2253
wood splitters

Hunter Enterprises Orillia Limited
P.O. Box 400
Orillia, Ontario, Canada
(705) 325-6111
circulating heaters, furnaces and boilers

Hydraform Products Corp.
P.O. Box 2409
Rochester, NH 03867
(603) 332-6128
heating stoves

Kickapoo Stove Works Standard: Takes 24'' log. Refractory firepot and welded steel plate body with cast iron doors.

Inglewood Stove Company
Rte. 4
Woodstock, VT 05091
(802) 457-3238
heating stoves

Isothermics, Inc.
P.O. Box 86
Augusta, NJ 07822
heat reclaimers

Jaxco, Inc.
P.O. Box B
Wautoma, WI 54982
insulated leather
fireplace gloves

Jernlund Products, Inc.
1620 Terrace Dr.
St. Paul, MN 55113

Kenenatics
1140 No. Parker Dr.
Janesville, WI 53545

Kickapoo Stove Works, Ltd.
Rte. 1-A
La Farge, WI 54639

Kickapoo Stove Works Boxer: Same construction as the Standard, 22' log length.

Knotty Wood Splitters
Hebron, CT 06248
(203) 228-9122
wood splitters

KNT, Inc.
P.O. Box 25
Hayesville, OH 44838
(419) 368-3241 or 368-8791
free-standing fireplaces
pre-fab fireplaces

Kristia Associates
P.O. Box 1118
Portland, ME 04104
(207) 772-2112

Jotul importers
heating stoves
free-standing fireplaces
pre-fabricated fireplaces

Lunenburg Foundry and Marine, Ltd.: The foundries of Nova Scotia, escpecially Lunenburg, are noted for traditional castings. Some are more advanced, many marine models are fitted for oil but can be had in coal, wood, and charcoal-burning models.

Lunenburg Foundry and Marine, Ltd.

La Font Corp.
1319 Town St.
Prentice, WI 54556
(715) 428-2881
fireplace accessories
wood splitters

Lance International
P.O. Box 562
1391 Blue Hills Ave.
Bloomfield, CT 06002
(203) 243-9700
fireplace accessories
heat reclaimers

W.F. Landers Co.
P.O. Box 211
Springfield, MA 01101
(413) 786-5722

Lassey Tools, Inc.
Plainville, CT 06062
(203) 747-2748
fireplace accessories

Newton Lee
Rte. 1 Box 116
Worcester, VT 05682
(802) 223-3119
fireplace accessories

Leyden Energy Conservation Corp.
Brattleboro Rd.
Leyden, MA 01337

Locke Stove Co.
114 West 11th St.
Kansas City, MO 64105
(816) 421-1650
heating stoves
circulating heaters

Log House Designs
Chatham, NH
(603) 694-3183
Fryeburg, ME 04058

Longwood Furnace Co.
Gallatin, MO 64640
furnaces

Louisville Tin and Stove Co.
P.O. Box 1079
Louisville, KY 40201
(502) 589-5380
heating stoves
stove accessories

Lunenburg Foundry and
Engineering Ltd.
Lunenburg
N.S. Canada BOJ 2CO
heating stoves for boat and home

Lynndale Manufacturing Company, Inc.
1309 North Hills Blvd.
Suite 207
North Little Rock, AR 72116
(501) 758-9602
P.O. Box 1154 Harrison, AR 72601
(501) 365-2378

Lunenburg Foundry and Marine, Ltd.

Lunenburg Foundry and Marine, Ltd.

Maine Wood Heat Co.
RD #1 Box 38
Norridgewock, ME 04957
(207) 696-5442

Majestic Company
Huntington, IN 46750
(219) 356-8000
free-standing fireplaces
pre-fab. fireplaces
fireplace accessories

Malleable Iron Range Co.
715 N. Spring St.
Beaver Dam, WI 53916
(414) 887-8131

Styria #130 woodburning cook range: firebrick lined, white enamel finish, nickeled fitting, 6½ gallon hot water tank.

Malm Fireplaces, Inc.
368 Yolanda Ave.
Santa Rosa, CA 95404
(707) 546-8955
free-standing fireplaces
pre-fab. fireplaces

Marathon Heater Co.
Box 165 RD2
Marathon, NY 13803

Marco Industries, Inc.
P.O. Box 6
Harrisonburg, VA 22801

Markade-Winnwood
4200 Birmingham Rd., NE
Kansas City, MO 64117
(816) 454-5260

heating stoves
furnaces and boilers
free-standing fireplaces
fireplace accessories
barrel stoves

Martin Industries
P.O. Box 730
Sheffield, AL 35660
(205) 383-2421

cookstove, heating stove, circulating heater, free-standing fireplace

Mechanical Product Development Corp.
Box 155
Swarthmore, PA 19081

Merry Music Box
20 McKown St.
Boothbay Harbor, ME 04538
(207) 633-2210

Styria heaters and cook-stoves

Metal Building Products, Inc.
35 Progress Ave.
Nashua, NH 03060
(603) 882-4271

circulating heaters
pre-fab fireplaces

Metal Concepts, Inc.
P.O. Box 25596
Seattle, WA 98125
(206) 365-3055

fireplace accessories

Styria Model 4 wood heater: firebrick lined, enamel finish, nickeled trim and doors.

Optimus Expedition 8R: a cased camping stove.

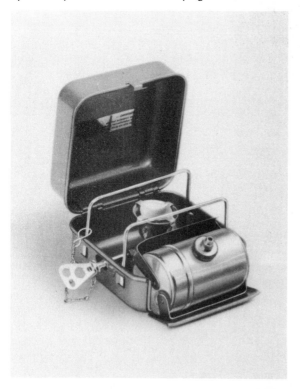

Optimus 731 "Mousetrap" pack stove: a recent design using pressurized flasks.

Modern-Aire
Modern Machine and Welding
Highway 2 West
Grand Rapids, MI 55744

Modern Kit Sales
P.O. Box 12501
N. Kansas City, MO 64116

Mohawk Industries, Inc.
173 Howland Ave.
Adams, MA 01220
(413) 743-3648
heating stoves-Tempwood

New England Fireplace Heaters, Inc.
372 Dorset St.
So. Burlington, VT 05401
(802) 658-4848
fireplace accessories

Newmac Mfg., Inc.
236 Norwich Ave.
Box 545
Woodstock, Ontario N4S 7W5, Canada
(519) 539-6147
furnaces and boilers

New Hampshire Wood Stoves, Inc.
Box 310
Plymouth, NH 03264

Nichols Environmental
5 Apple Rd.
Beverly, MA 01915

Nortech Corporation
300 Greenwood Ave.
Midland Park, NJ 07432
(201) 445-6900
wood splitters

Old Country Appliances
P.O. Box 330
Vacaville, CA 95688

cooking stoves
Tirolia importers

Optimus-Princess
Box 3448
Santa Fe Springs, CA 90670

camping stoves

Pioneer Lamps and Stoves
71 Yesler Way
Pioneer Sq. Station
Seattle, WA 98104
cook stoves

Portland Stove Foundry
57 Kennebec St.
P.O. Box 1156
Portland, ME 04104
(207) 773-0256

cook stoves, heating stoves, circulating heaters, free-
standing fireplace, fireplace accessories, barrel stove

Optimus Svea 123R backpacking stove: burns white gas;
stamped and machined brass; a tiny piece of sculpture.

Optimus OO: collapsible kerosene pack stove of proven
design.

Preston Distributing Co.
10 Whidden St.
Lowell, MA 01852
(617) 458-6303
Poele Importer, circulating heaters

Preway, Inc.
Wisconsin Rapids, WI 54494
(715) 423-1100
free-standing fireplaces, pre-fab fire place

Quaker Stove Co.
Box 41
Line Lexington, PA 18932

U.S. Stove Company Sheeprancher Cookstove: not airtight but endearing; wood or soft coal.

Radiant Grate
31 Morgan Park
Clinton, CT 06413
(203) 669-6250
fireplace accessories

Ram and Forge
Brooks, ME 04921
(207) 722-3379
heating stoves
furnaces and boilers

REM Industries
408 C Simms Bldg.
Dayton, OH 45402

Ridgeway Steel Fabricators, Inc.
Box 382
Bark St.
Ridgeway, PA 15853
(814) 776-1323 or 776-6156
pre-fabricated fireplace
fireplace accessories

Riteway Manufacturing Co.
P.O. Box 6
Harrisonburg, VA 22801
(703) 434-7090
heating stoves, circulating heaters, furnaces and boilers

Riteway airtights in several models and capacities. (model #37 shown). The search for the last percentage point of efficiency and hang fashion.

Ro Knich Products, Inc.
P.O. Box 311-E
No. Chicago, IL 60064

S & A Distributors
730 Midtown Plaza
Syracuse, NY 13210

Scandinavian Stoves, Inc.
Box 72
Alstead, NH 03602
cook stoves
heating stoves

Scot's Stove Co.
11 Ells St.
Norwalk, CT 06850
heating stoves

SEVCA, in Standard and Baby models, ingeniously fabricated of recycled propane tanks. Available with optional water-heating coil; and undeniably efficient unit. As homely and appealing as a VW bug.

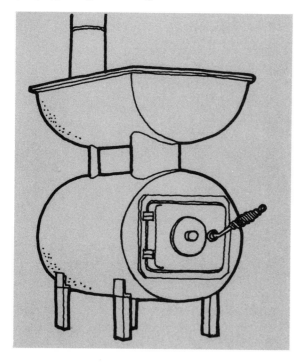

Shipmate Skippy Stove: Shipmate manufactures marine stoves for yachts and fishing boats of all sizes.

Self Sufficiency Products
1 Appletree Square
Minneapolis, MN 55420

SEVCA Stove Works
Box 396
Bellows Falls, VT 05101
heating stoves

Seymour Mfg. Co.
500 N. Broadway
Seymour, IN 47274
fireplace accessories

Shenandoah Manufacturing Co., Inc.
Box 839
Harrisonburg, VA 22801
(703) 434-3838
heating stoves, circulating heaters, fireplace accessories

Shipmate Stoves
Richmond King Co.
Souderton, PA 18964
boat stoves

Sierra Stoveworks of Elmira
RD 1
Elmira, NY 14903
plate stepstove

John P. Smith
174 Cedar St.
Branford, CT 06405
(203) 488-7225

Solar Sauna
Box 466
Hollis, NH 03049

Sotz Corporation
23797 Sprague Rd.
Columbia Station, OH 44028

Southeastern Vermont Community
Action SEVCA
7-9 Westminster Street
Bellows Falls, VT 05101
(802) 463-4447

an efficient barrel stove with a half-barrel heat exchanger
above it that is welded up from recycled propane tanks;
two sizes

#206 CH Shipmate Cabin Heater: Stainless steel, heavy cast
iron firebox.

Southport Stoves
Howell Corporation
248 Tolland Street
East Hartford, CT 06108
(203) 289-6079

Morsø, Efel, and Surdiac importer; heating stoves and
free-standing fireplaces, stove and woodcutting accessories

Sturges Heat Recovery, Inc.
P.O. Box 397
Stone Ridge, NY 12484
(914) 687-0281

fireplace accessories
heat reclaimer

Suburban Manufacturing Company
4700 Forest Drive
Box 6472
Columbia, SC 29206
(803) 782-2649
circulating heaters

Sunshine Stove Works
RD 1 Box 38
Norridgewock, ME 04957
(914) 887-4580
heating stoves

Superior Fireplace Corporation
Mobex Corporation
Box 2066
Fullerton, CA 92633
fireplaces, pre-fab

Surdiac-Gotha 511. A French coal burner imported along with other models of less strenuous design by Southport Stoves.

Taos Equipment Manufacturers, Inc.
Box 1565
Taos, NM 87571
(505) 758-8253
wood splitters

Tekton Design Corp.
Conway, MA 01341
(413) 369-4685
Tasso and Kedelfabric-Tarm importer, furnaces and boilers

Temco
Box 1184
Nashville, NH 37202
(615) 297-7551
free-standing and pre-fab fireplaces

Thermo-Matic
Rt. 145, Lawyersville Road
Cobleskill, NY 12043

Timberline Productions
110 E. First St.
E. Syracuse, NY 13057

Timberline Stoves
RFD #1, 12 Columbia Dr.
Amherst, NH 03031
heating stoves

Upland Model 17 Airtight. At first glance the Upland designs seem remarkably familiar, but they do differ in salient ways from the better-known originals.

Upland Stove Co., Inc.
P.O. Box 87
Greene, NY 13778
heating stoves

Vaporpack, Incorporated
Box 428
Exeter, NH 03833
(603) 778-0509
heat reclaimers

Veneered Metals, Inc.
Box 327
Edison, NJ 08817
stoveboard

Vermont Castings Defiant Parlor Stove: Combination fireplace/airtight. Much copied, it remains unequaled in its excellent design and attention to manufacturing detail. Side and front loading.

Vermont Downdrafter by Vermont Woodstove Co.

Vermont Castings, Incorporated
Box 126
Prince Street
Randolph, VT 05060
(802) 728-3355
the superb Vigilant and Defiant stoves

Vermont Counterflow Wood Furnace
Plainfield, VT 05667
furnaces

Vermont Energy Products
100 Broad Street
Lyndonville, VT 05851
(802) 626-8842

Vermont Iron Stove Works, Inc.
The Bobbin Mill
Warren, VT 05674
(802) 496-2821
heating stoves

Vermont Soapstone Co.
Perkinsville, VT 05151
heating stoves and accessories

Vermont Techniques, Incorporated
Box 107
Northfield, VT 05663
(802) 485-7905
fireplace accessories

Vermont Woodstove Company
307 Elm Street
Bennington, VT 05201
(802) 442-3985
heating stoves

E.G. Wasburne & Company
83 Andover Street
Danvers, MA 01923

Washington Stove Works
Box 687
3402 Smith Street
Everett, WA 98201

cooking and heating stoves, circulating heaters, free-standing fireplaces, barrel stove kits and fireplace accessories

Woodburning Specialties
P.O. Box 5
No. Marshfield, MA 02059

Hunter Importer
circulating heaters and furnaces

Waterford Ironfounders Limited
Waterford, Ireland
Waterford 5911

cooking stoves

Warmglow Products, Inc.
625 Century
Grand Rapids, MI 49503

heating stoves

White Mesa, Incorporated
110 Laguna
Albuquerque, NM 87104
(505) 247-1066

Vigilant by Vermont Castings: A more compact combination fireplace/airtight. Top and Front loading. These two stoves, disguised in restrained traditional designs, are among the most technologically advanced and livable stoves available now.

Whitten Enterprises
Arlington, VT 05250

Whittier Steel & Manufacturing Co.
10725 South Painter Avenue
Sante Fe Springs, CA 90670

Whole Earth Access Company
2466 Shattuck Avenue
Berkeley, CA 94704
(415) 848-0510
stoves, lamps, barrel stoves

Yankee Woodstoves Model 30—a low cost alternative, it is available with several options or in kit form. Yankee Woodstoves also offers other models.

Wilson Industries
2296 Wycliff
St. Paul, MN 55114
(612) 646-7214
furnaces

Worcester Brush Co.
38 Austin St.
Worcester, MA 01601
chimney sweeping brushes

Yankee Woodstoves
Cross St.
Bennington, NH 03442
(603) 588-6358
heating stoves

ODE TO A STOVE

A mother, large & warm
Lighting the corner of the room . . .
Spreading heat & comfort
Almost to the hall.
We come rushing in:
    Blue Fingers, Red Noses
From various places:
    Icy Ears and sub-zero toeses,
To thaw ourselves before this
    Mother Stove
Whose vast form emanates
Our word for love.

                translated from the Chinese by
                Jossie Nash

A great deal of gratitude is due to many friends who gave time and advice to this book: Russell Peck and Harriet of Bow and Arrow Stove Company gave their broad knowledge and references, Duncan Syme of Vermont Castings gave his thoughts and a keen sense of grammar, Doug Cain of the Manchester Stove and Tin Museum gave his fellowship and some wonderful corn pie, Bob Cawley of Cawley-LeMay gave good advice and good humor, Lew Gillensen of Everest House gave unfailing grace to an oversensitive author, and Trina Schart Hyman did *not* give me the promised pornographic picture of her and her kitchen stove, for which I thank her.

ASHEVILLE-BUNCOMBE TECHNICAL COLLEGE

3 3312 00001 6055

TH
7438
.A3
1978

80-688

Adkins, Jan

The art and ingenu-
ity of the woodstove

Asheville-Buncombe Technical College
LEARNING RESOURCES CENTER
340 Victoria Road
Asheville, North Carolina 28801